Bridging 5 to 6

Summer SPLASH

LEARNING ACTIVITIES

Brighter Child®
An imprint of Carson-Dellosa Publishing LLC
Greensboro, North Carolina

Brighter Child®
An imprint of Carson-Dellosa Publishing LLC
P.O. Box 35665
Greensboro, NC 27425 USA

03-137131151

Table of Contents

Making the Most of
Summer Splash Learning Activities

This resource contains a myriad of fun and challenging reading and math activities. The reading pages provide practice in reading for details, drawing conclusions, compare and contrast, and similes and metaphors. The math pages review skills taught in fifth grade, such as multiplication and division, fractions and decimals, and problem solving.

Most of the activities in the book are designed so that your child can work independently. However, your child will enjoy the activities much more if you work alongside him or her. Make sure to let your child know that this is not a workbook with tests, but a book of fun activities that you can do together. The book is divided into 10 weeks, with about eight activity pages per week. Feel free to choose how many per day and in which order you do the activities, but complete the weeks in sequence, since activities become increasingly challenging as the book progresses.

Summer Splash Learning Activities provides an important link between your child's fifth and sixth-grade school years. It reviews what your child learned in fifth grade, providing the confidence and skills that he or she needs for the coming fall. The activities in this book will help your child successfully bridge the gap between fifth and sixth grade by reviewing and reinforcing the important and essential skills for his or her continued academic success. These activities are designed to

- review skills in math, reading, and language arts that your child learned the previous year.

- give you an opportunity to monitor your child's skills in various areas.

- offer you a chance to spend special time with your child.

- enable your child to continue routine daily learning activities.

- give you a chance to praise your child's efforts.

- demonstrate to your child that you value lifetime learning.

- make you an active and important part of your child's educational development.

Getting Started

In order for your child to get the most from the activities in this resource, use these helpful tips to make these learning experiences interesting and, most of all, fun!

- Set aside a time each day for completing the activities. Make it a time when your child will be most ready to learn, and make it a routine.
- Provide a pleasant, quiet place to work. This means no TV in your child's work area. Also, make sure there is a sufficient light source.
- Review in advance the activity page(s) your child will complete that session. This way, you will be able to familiarize yourself with the lesson.
- Have your child read the directions aloud beforehand to make sure he or she understands the activity. Instructions are written for the child, but he or she may need your help reading and/or understanding them.
- Let your child help choose which activity he or she would like to complete that day.
- Praise all your child's work. It's the effort, not necessarily the end result, that counts most.

No one knows better than you how your child learns best, so use this book to enhance the way you already work with him or her. Use every opportunity possible as a learning experience, whether making a trip through the grocery store or riding in the car. Pose problems and let your child figure out how to solve them, asking questions such as *Which route should we take to the park? What could we use to make a plant grow straight?* or *How high should we hang this shelf?* Also, respond excitedly to discoveries your child makes throughout the day with comments such as *That rock is really unique! I wonder how long it took the spider to spin that web;* or *You spent your money wisely.* In this way, you will encourage and motivate your child to learn throughout the day and for the rest of his or her life, providing the confidence and self-esteem he or she needs for continued academic success.

Everyday Learning Activities

Use these simple educational activities to keep your child's mind engaged and active during the summer months and all year long!

- Ask your child to make a schedule of events for the day, in the order in which they will take place. Ask him or her to prioritize the list and number the events.

- On a neighborhood walk or while driving in the car, encourage your child to read all the street signs and numbers.

- Read with your child each day. Encourage your child to retell the story to you. Then, have him or her make up original adventures for the story characters or write an additional chapter.

- Have your child write down important dates such as family birthdays, important trips or outings, or holidays. Be sure your child capitalizes the name of the month and week and uses a comma between the day and year.

- During a visit to the park or playground, invite your child to describe what he or she sees there, using as many adjectives as possible.

- Have your child list three things you can smell, feel, taste, or see in a particular room of the house or on a "senses walk."

- Have your child identify as many parts of the human body as he or she can. Ask him or her to describe the function of each part, if possible.

- Ask your child to read a recipe with you for a simple dish. Practice measuring skills by simulating measuring out the ingredients with water or rice in measuring spoons or cups.

- Have your child read the price of items in a store or supermarket. Challenge him or her to estimate how much can be bought with a designated amount of money. Can your child figure out how much change is left over?

- Encourage your child to tell you whether certain objects in your home (sofa, pencil) would be measured in pounds or ounces.

- Fill a measuring cup with water to different levels, and invite your child to read the measurement and then write it as a fraction.

- Encourage your child to read nonfiction library books and make up creative stories about the subject matter (e.g., lions or airplanes).

6

Assessment

Read the following passage and answer questions 1–8.

We are destroying our personal link to the future. How can that be? It is disintegrating because we do not write. Think for a moment about how we know about the personal lives of the people who lived before our time. We know what these people did, ate, saw, wore, and believed, because they wrote about it. Throughout history, people have left records of their lives. Some wrote letters to loved ones who lived far away. Pioneers kept diaries and journals that depicted their treacherous, sometimes deadly journey as they trudged across the United States in search of better lives. Soldiers wrote letters home describing the horrors of war. The words of our ancestors have survived the years, and as we read their accounts, we see a glimpse of what their lives were like.

Today, with the advent of new technology, writing has become less common. Instead, many people communicate via phone, e-mail, or text message. Our words disappear as soon as they are spoken or deleted. If we want future generations to know about the lives we've lived, we need to leave a written legacy. It's up to each of you. Pick up a pen and write a letter to a friend or family member. Start a diary or a journal and record what you do each day. These events may seem trivial to you, but they might hold great insight for your descendents. Imagine your great-great-great-grandchild reading your journal more than 100 years from now and enjoying what you wrote. Start today. Write. Create your own personal link to the future.

1. What is the main idea?_____

2. List three details that support the main idea. _____

   _____

   _____

3. Look up the word *link* in a dictionary. Write two meanings for this word.

   _____

   _____

Assessment

4. Underline the part of the following sentence that is the cause. Draw a box around the part of the sentence that is the effect.

We will not have a personal link to the future if we do not write.

5. What is the author's purpose? _____

6. *Down-to-earth* is an idiom that describes a type of person. What do you think it means?

_____

_____

7. Summarize the article. _____

_____

_____

_____

_____

8. Compare and contrast something else that we do differently from our ancestors. Draw and fill in a Venn diagram to depict the similarities and differences.

Assessment

Read the following passage and answer questions 9–13

"Let's see . . . 25, 50, 75, 80, 81, 82 . . . . That's $47.82," counted Cal. He gathered the change and placed it next to the bills on the red comforter. Then, he flopped back onto the bed, making the change bounce.

"Rats! We still need $12.18 to cover the admission cost," pouted Leo. "Mom said that we have to have the total cost of admission before we can go to the Greatest Theme Park Ever." The two lay on the floor in Cal's room, imagining the theme park: great junk food like chili dogs, cotton candy, frozen drinks, and elephant ears; games that offer prizes of oversized stuffed animals; and the rides, oh, the rides—wild roller coasters, spinning swings, and Ferris wheels!

"We won't have enough money with our allowances for two more weeks," said Cal. "Besides, that doesn't leave anything for food or souvenirs."

"I know," Leo said, "and I've already checked between the couch cushions, under the car seats, and in all of our jacket pockets." The two sat in mutual gloom. They watched the colorful leaves drop outside the window. Suddenly, they had an idea.

9. Which of the following events happens next to last?

A. The boys have an idea.

B. The boys watch the leaves drop outside.

C. The boys count their money.

10. List three things the boys would like do at the amusement park. _____

_____

_____

11. What is the setting of the story?_____

12. What idea do you think the boys have at the end of the story? _____

_____

13. Do you think that the boys are brothers? _____

Circle the detail in the story that supports your answer.

9

Assessment Analysis

Answer Key:
1. People today should write more to provide a link for future generations of people.
2. Answers will vary, but may include: Throughout history, people have left written records of their lives. Some people wrote letters to loved ones far away. Pioneers kept diaries and journals. Soldiers wrote about the horrors of war. Writing has become less common with the advent of new technology.
3. A relationship between people, events, or situations that connects them in some way; A ring or piece of a chain
4. cause—if we do not write; effect—we will not have a personal link to the future.
5. to persuade readers to write
6. Answers will vary, but should include the idea that someone who is down-to-earth is not pretentious or arrogant.
7.-8. Answers will vary.
9. B.
10. The boys would eat junk food, play games, and ride amusement-park rides.
11. The boys' home
12. The boys will rake leaves to earn the extra money that they need.
13. yes; they have the same mother.

Check assessment answers using the answer key. Match the questions with incorrect answers to the sections. To provide extra practice in problem areas, refer to the pages listed under each section.

Number(s)	Skill	Activity Page(s)
1., 2.	main idea and supporting details	14–17
3.	multiple-meaning words	22–23
4.	cause and effect	24–25
5.	author's viewpoint and word choice	65
6.	understanding idioms	30–31
7.	summarizing	38–41
8.	interpreting a Venn diagram	32–33
9.	sequencing	46–49
10., 13.	reading for details	54–57, 62–64, 70–73
11.	story elements	78–81
12., 13.	making inferences and predicting outcomes	86–89

Assessment

Write the value of each underlined digit.

1. 8,2<u>3</u>4   26,3<u>8</u>4   <u>2</u>88,403   <u>1</u>,643,522

_____   _____   _____   _____

Estimate each sum or difference.

2.   32   789   8,286   4,015
       + 17   + 212   – 1,323   + 2,675

Solve.

3. (12 + 8) – (4 + 12) = _____   8 + (7 – 3) = (10 + 2) + _____

4. 1,214   5,004 $x + 4 = 16$ $n – 8 = 12$
      2,003   – 324 $x =$ _____ $n =$ _____
        468
      + 92

5. $6.25   832$\overline{)3,736}$ $y \times 3 = 27$ $36 \div j = 9$
      x 329 $y =$ _____ $j =$ _____

Fill in each blank.

6. 1 mile = _____ ft.   4,000 lb. = _____ tons
7. 1 mile = _____ yd.   1 gal. = _____ qt.
8. 1 m = _____ dm   1 km = _____ m
9. 1 kg = _____ g   12 c. = _____ p.

Solve. Reduce or simplify if needed.

10. $1\frac{1}{5} + 2\frac{3}{5} =$ ____ $5\frac{6}{9} – 2\frac{3}{9} =$ ____ $3\frac{3}{4} \times 5\frac{2}{3} =$ ____ $4\frac{1}{2} \div 1\frac{1}{3} =$ ____

11.   23.14   44   3.2   0.46$\overline{)82.8}$
        + 1.006   – 0.17   x 4.6

11

Assessment

Draw an example of each figure.

12.   Line AB   Segment ST   Ray CD

Classify each angle as acute, right, obtuse, or straight.

13.

_____   _____   _____   _____

Draw an isosceles triangle.   **Draw a right triangle.**

14.   **15.**

Find the perimeter and area of the figure.

16. P = _____ in.   4 in.

17. A = _____ sq. in

7 in.

Write the ratio in 3 different ways.

18. 4 cats to 6 dogs

_____

_____

_____

Find the mean, median, and mode for each set of data. Round to the nearest tenth.

19. 2, 8, 6, 4, 5, 3, 2, 4

mean = _____

median = _____

mode = _____

20.   45, 45, 70, 40, 60, 42, 42, 60, 42

mean = _____

median = _____

mode = _____

Solve.

21. The sixth graders at Jackson Elementary School read 682 books. The rest of the school read 5,972 books. The students missed their goal by 96 books. The goal was to read how many books?   _____ books

Assessment Analysis

Answer Key:
1. 200; 80; 200,000; 1,000,000
2. 50; 1,000; 7,000; 7,000
3. 4, 0
4. 3,777; 4,680; 12; 20
5. $2,056.25; 4 r408; 9; 4
6. 5,280; 2
7. 1,760; 4
8. 10; 1,000
9. 1,000; 6
10. $3\frac{3}{5}$, $3\frac{1}{3}$, $21\frac{1}{4}$, $3\frac{3}{8}$
11. 24.146; 43.83; 14.72; 180
12.
13. right, straight, acute, obtuse
14. should have 2 equal sides
15. should have 1 right angle
16. 22
17. 28
18. 46 ; 4:6; 4 to 6
19. 4.3; 4; 2 and 4
20. 49.6; 45; 42
21. 6,750 books

After reviewing the assessment, match the problems answered incorrectly to the corresponding activity pages. Your child should spend extra time on those activities to strengthen math skills.

Number(s)	Skill	Activity Page(s)
1.	numeration	18–19
2., 3., 4.	addition and subtraction	26–29
5.	multiplication and division	34–37
6., 7., 8., 9.	measurement	20–21
10., 11.	fractions and decimals	42–45, 50–53, 58–61
12., 13., 14., 15., 16., 17.	geometry	66–69
18.	ratio and percent	74–77
19., 20.	probability and statistics	82–85
21.	problem solving	90–92

Rocks in the Head

The **main idea** identifies the main point (or points) in a passage. Each paragraph of a passage has a **topic sentence,** which tells the main idea of the paragraph and supports the main idea of the passage. All of the details in a paragraph are clues to help you understand the topic sentence and main idea. These clues are called **supporting details.**

All four topic sentences refer to the same main idea: rocks. The supporting details are listed separately. Match each detail to the appropriate topic sentence.

1. Rocks can be found in many places.

_____   _____

2. Rocks have many uses.

_____   _____

3. There are three different types of rocks.

_____   _____

4. Various forces weather rocks.

_____   _____

A. Water washes away bits and pieces of rock.
B. Sedimentary rock is formed underwater as millions of years worth of mud, pebbles, and other objects are pressed together and solidified.
C. Ground rocks are mixed together with an adhering agent to make concrete.
D. Mountains are comprised of enormous sheets of rock.
E. Bedrock is located below soil.
F. Bedrock provides stability for homes and other structures.
G. Changes in temperature cause cracks to develop in rocks.
H. Igneous rock is produced from hardened magma and lava.

Turn Up the Power

Read the passage.

The ability to do work is called *energy*. Machines need energy, or fuel, to work. This energy can come from many sources. Fossil fuels, like coal, gas, and oil, are one important source of energy. They come from the earth and are used to fuel power plants, automobiles, and other machines. Another source of energy is wind. Wind can power windmills. It can also be converted into electricity, push gears to grind grains, or be used to pump water. Water is also a key source of energy. Dams are used to harness energy from rivers and convert it into electricity. Scientists are researching the possibility of using ocean waves and tides for energy. Finally, there is the sun, or solar energy. Solar cells can turn sunlight to electricity, which can then be used to power cars and electrical devices and heat homes. Although fossil fuels are currently used the most, other energy sources are becoming more commonly used and research is being done to make those energy sources more effective and economical.

Write the topic and main idea on the lines. Then, list four major supporting details. Choose two minor supporting details for each major detail and list them.

Topic: _____

Main idea: _____

1. Major supporting detail: _____
   A. Minor supporting detail: _____
   B. Minor supporting detail: _____
2. Major supporting detail: _____
   A. Minor supporting detail: _____
   B. Minor supporting detail: _____
3. Major supporting detail: _____
   A. Minor supporting detail: _____
   B. Minor supporting detail: _____
4. Major supporting detail: _____
   A. Minor supporting detail: _____
   B. Minor supporting detail: _____

Vertebrates

Read the passage.

Vertebrates are animals that have backbones. Animals that do not have backbones are called invertebrates, or "not vertebrates." There are five different kinds of vertebrates: amphibians, birds, fish, mammals, and reptiles. Each type has distinct characteristics. Some are warm-blooded, while others are cold-blooded. Body coverings, habitats, methods of reproduction, and methods of breathing differ from one to another. The one characteristic that all vertebrates—no matter what shape or size—share is a skeletal structure with a backbone.

Amphibians are cold-blooded, skin-covered vertebrates. They have two distinct parts to their life cycles. The adult female lays jellylike eggs that hatch into water creatures. Infant and juvenile amphibians have gills and spend their time in fluid environments. When they become adults, a transition is made—gills make way for lungs—and they spend most of their time on land. Although adult amphibians must breathe air, many often need water to stay moist. Frogs and salamanders are common examples of amphibians.

Like amphibians, birds can live around water. In fact, penguins are more comfortable in water than on land. Some of these feathered creatures, like kingfishers, even eat amphibians. Birds also live on nearly every type of land feature, and the majority of birds spend much of their time airborne. Not all birds fly, but all birds are covered with feathers. Unlike amphibians, birds are warm-blooded. They breathe with lungs from the moment that they hatch from brittle-shelled eggs. When they are born, baby birds are helpless. Without parental care, both while in the egg and after hatching, they will not survive.

Fish are lifelong water creatures. These cold-blooded animals are covered with scales and use gills to extract oxygen from the water. Most fish, like salmon, come from jellylike eggs, but a few, such as guppies, develop inside the mother and are born alive. Fish generally do not care for their young.

Mammals are the only vertebrates whose females produce milk to feed their young. Nearly all mammals give birth to live young. They breathe with lungs and are warm-blooded, and most are covered with hair or fur. Because they are warm-blooded, mammals must make their own heat, which requires additional energy and fuel in the form of food. Mammals have developed many ways to retain heat, such as thicker hair and

Vertebrates

fur in the winter months, layers of fat under the skin, and, in the case of humans, artificial coverings like clothing. Other examples of mammals include seals, rats, kangaroos, tigers, elephants, and dogs.

Although most mammals are land creatures, there is a group of ocean-dwelling mammals. Many of these mammals are members of the whale family, such as orcas, porpoises, humpbacks, and dolphins. They live in a fluid environment and can hold their breath for long periods of time, but they, too, have lungs and must surface to breathe.

Reptiles are the final group of vertebrates. They are cold-blooded like amphibians and fish. They also lay eggs. Reptiles are covered with scales; some scales form shells, like those of the turtle and tortoise groups. Reptiles lay leathery eggs, and they breathe with lungs. Turtles, alligators, and crocodiles spend much of their time in the water, but they are often found resting on logs or on shore, warming themselves in the sun.

Write the main idea in the top oval. Write the five major details in the next set of ovals. Finally, write two minor details that support each of the five major details in the rectangles.

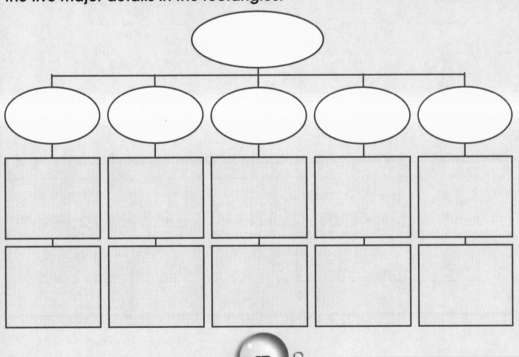

Place Value

Study the chart below. The underlined digit 6 is in the hundred thousands place. So, it has a value of 600,000.

Billions			Millions			Thousands			Ones		
Hundred Billions	Ten Billions	Billions	Hundred Millions	Ten Millions	Millions	Hundred Thousands	Ten Thousands	Thousands	Hundreds	Tens	Ones
		5,	5	0	3,	6	7	3,	9	8	2

Study the example above. Then, write the value of each underlined digit.

1. 2,8<u>4</u>3

   5,<u>7</u>01

   6<u>2</u>,483

2. 13,90<u>5</u>

   3,<u>8</u>73,452

   4<u>7</u>3,206,311

3. 7<u>9</u>,337

   <u>6</u>38,317

   <u>7</u>,741,412

4. 878,<u>3</u>04

   7<u>4</u>8,244,862

   98,4<u>2</u>3,648

5. 458,2<u>3</u>1

   <u>9</u>81,324,109

   <u>1</u>,346,225

6. Write two 12-digit numbers so that one is exactly 10 billion more than the other.

Changing the Place Value

Change the 8 in 48,233 to 6. The new number is 46,233.
The number was decreased by 2,000.

Study the example above. Then, change the digit indicated for each problem. Circle the amount that the entire number changed.

1. Change the 5 in 25,136 to 7. How much more is the new number?

7	2
2,000	7,000

2. Change the 8 in 28,496 to 3. How much less is the new number?

5	8
5,000	3,000

3. Change the 3 in 173,286 to 5. How much more is the new number?

200	2,000
20	2

4. Change the 2 in 6,200,436 to 5. How much more is the new number?

3	200,000
300,000	5,00,000

5. Change the 6 in 4,358,617 to 2. How much less is the new number?

40	4
400	2

6. Change the 8 in 87,362 to 3. How much less is the new number?

5,000,000	5
3	50,000

7. Change the 2 in 207,314 to 8. How much more is the new number?

8,000	800,000
6,000	600,000

8. Change the 6 in 860,429 to 1. How much less is the new number?

5	50,000
60,000	1

9. Change the 4 in 6,040,328 to 9. How much more is the new number?

5,000,000	500
90	50,000

10. Change the 5 in 873,295 to 3. How much less is the new number?

2	20,000
30,000	5

Length in the Standard System

These are equivalent measurements of **length** in the **standard** system.	1 foot = 12 inches 1 yard = 3 feet 1 mile = 5,280 feet

When changing from a smaller unit to a larger unit (in. to ft.), divide.
When changing from a larger unit to a smaller unit (ft. to in.), multiply.

Study the equivalent measurements above. Then, change each measurement to inches.

1. 3 ft.

_____ in.

4 yd.

_____ in.

2 ft. 4 in.

_____ in.

9 yd.

_____ in.

2. 5 yd. 1 ft.

_____ in.

120 ft.

_____ in.

8 yd.

_____ in.

10 ft. 7 in.

_____ in.

Change each measurement to feet.

3. 6 yd.

_____ ft.

2 mi.

_____ ft.

72 in.

_____ ft.

3 yd. 1 ft.

_____ ft.

4. 48 in.

_____ ft.

5 yd. 2 ft.

_____ ft.

$1\frac{1}{2}$ mi.

_____ ft.

96 in.

_____ ft.

Write each measurement as yards and feet.

5. 37 ft.

_____ yd.
_____ ft.

84 in.

_____ yd.
_____ ft.

22 ft.

_____ yd.
_____ ft.

5 ft. 24 in.

_____ yd.
_____ ft.

Write each measurement as feet and inches.

6. 28 in.

_____ ft.
_____ in.

45 in.

_____ ft.
_____ in.

$6\frac{1}{4}$ yd.

_____ ft.
_____ in.

6 yd. 30 in.

_____ ft.
_____ in.

Length in the Metric System

These are equivalent measurements of **length** in the **metric** system.	1 centimeter (cm)	= 10 millimeters (mm)
	1 decimeter (dm)	= 10 centimeters (cm)
	1 meter (m)	= 10 decimeters (dm)
	1 kilometer (km)	= 1,000 meters (m)

Measure each segment to the nearest centimeter.

1. _____ ▬

2. _____ ▬▬▬▬▬▬▬▬▬▬▬▬▬

3. _____ ▬▬▬▬▬▬▬

4. _____ ▬▬▬

5. _____ ▬▬▬▬▬▬▬▬▬

Study the equivalent measures above. Then, complete each sentence.

6. 7 km = _____ m   16 cm = _____ mm   8 m = _____ cm

7. 11 m = _____ dm   5,000 m = _____ km   700 cm = _____ m

8. 40 mm = _____ cm   12 km = _____ m   _____ m = 800 cm

9. _____ cm = 17 dm   3.5 m = _____ cm   _____ m = 6.8 km

10. Choose the most sensible measurement.

width of a dollar bill   width of a house

7 cm   7 m   7 km   12 cm   12 dm   12 m

Looking It Up

Words often have more than one dictionary meaning. The **context** of a passage determines a word's meaning.

Circle the best meaning for each boldfaced word.

1. The **last** tooth that Will lost was an eyetooth. Now, a bicuspid is loose.
   A. the final one
   B. the previous one
   C. the one that endures

2. The hamster looked cold. Selena decided to **line** its box with cotton.
   A. to cover the inner surface
   B. a short letter
   C. the straight two-dimensional figure between two points

3. The smell of freshly **ground** coffee was wafting through the house. "It smells good," thought Jamal. "It's too bad it tastes so awful."
   A. a basis for a belief
   B. the surface of the earth
   C. smashed into small bits

4. Ainslee was studying a honeycomb **cell.** It was incredible to look at it with a magnifying glass.
   A. a small protoplasmic portion of a living organism
   B. a small compartment
   C. the smallest unit of an organization

5. The movie was **over.** It was time to go to bed.
   A. finished
   B. in a position above
   C. to move from a vertical to a horizontal position

6. The test was nearly over. Kyle was trying to **rack** his brain for an answer to the second question. He just could not come up with one.
   A. to think under emotional stress
   B. to fly in high wind
   C. a framework on which things are placed

22

Play Ball

Even small words can lead to confusion when they have more than one meaning.

Read the paragraph. Use the context to determine the meanings of the bold words. Circle the letter next to each correct definition.

Mia was getting ready to **bat**. She **planted** her feet in the **box** and got ready to **swing**. Kim threw a **strike** across home **plate**. The next two pitches were **balls**. Mia connected with the last **pitch** and ran to first **base**. She hit in the winning **run**.

1. bat
   A. a flying mammal
   B. to take a turn at bat
   C. a stick used to hit a ball

2. planted
   A. dug a hole and placed a seed in the ground
   B. a factory or workshop
   C. fixed in place

3. box
   A. a cardboard rectangular prism
   B. an area next to home plate
   C. to punch another person

4. swing
   A. to move a stick toward a ball
   B. a type of music
   C. a seat attached to two chains

5. strike
   A. a pitch that crosses the plate within a certain range
   B. to hit forcefully
   C. to delete something

6. plate
   A. to coat with metal
   B. a circular object that holds food
   C. a square on the ground used to mark a base

7. balls
   A. pitches thrown that do not pass within a certain range
   B. spherical objects
   C. large, formal gatherings

8. pitch
   A. a musical tone
   B. a ball thrown to a batter
   C. to fall headlong

9. base
   A. the bottom part of an object
   B. one of the four stations on a ball field
   C. lowly or vile

10. run
    A. to move legs rapidly
    B. to move in a melted state
    C. a score made after reaching home plate

One after Another

Read each paragraph. Then, answer the questions.

Tien was sitting on the swing. Juan walked up behind him. Juan grabbed the swing in both hands and pulled as he backed up. He pushed as he ran forward, let go of the swing, and ducked under the swing as it soared into the air. Tien rode up into the air, and came whooshing back down. He used his legs to pump and continued swinging in the back and forth arc.

1. What causes Tien to go forward? _____

2. What is the effect of Tien's going forward? _____

Jan set her lunch bag on the bus seat. She turned around to talk to a friend and bumped the bag onto the floor. Her apple rolled four seats forward, and her popcorn spilled into a white puddle. Jan watched as her drink bottle bounced three times and then exploded.

3. What causes Jan's lunch to hit the floor? _____

4. What is the effect of the bottle bouncing three times? _____

Write and answer one cause question and one effect question for the following paragraph.

Pablo set his alarm for 7:30 A.M. so that he would have a half hour to finish his homework in the morning. He went to sleep. That night, there was a thunderstorm. The power went out for five minutes and then came back on. The next morning, Pablo's mom called for him at 8:00. Pablo couldn't believe it. His alarm had not gone off. He had to rush to get ready for school and finish his homework.

5. _____

_____

6. _____

_____

Friendly Conversation

In a **conversation,** what one person says affects the other person's response. There is a cause-and-effect relationship.

Read Riley's one-sided dialogue. Think about what Tyler would say based upon what Riley says. Then, fill in the missing dialogue.

Riley: Hi, Tyler. Will you help me with this math problem?

Tyler: _____
Riley: Yeah, I'd love to play tag when we're finished.

Tyler: _____
Riley: It's this one: 3,405 minus 2,673.

Tyler: _____
Riley: Well, I keep getting 1,272 as the answer. But, when I add it to 2,673, I get 3,945—not 3,405. I know that it's wrong.

Tyler: _____
Riley: Yeah, it is frustrating.

Tyler: _____
Riley: Oh, that's right. I can't take 7 from 0 and still get 7.

Tyler: _____
Riley: I know; we won't give up. Can you look over this again?

Tyler: _____
Riley: The hundreds?

Tyler: _____
Riley: I see. I can't subtract 6 from the 3 that I have left from regrouping the hundreds to the tens. I have to regroup the thousands to the hundreds, also.

Tyler: _____
Riley: Now, I get 732. I can add that to 2,673, and I get 3,405! We did it! Thanks, Tyler.

Tyler: _____
Riley: Yeah, let's put this away and go outside.

25

Addition With and Without Regrouping

1. Add the **ones** column. Regroup as needed.	2. Add the **tens** column. Regroup as needed.	3. Add the **hundreds** column. Regroup as needed.

¹
796
+ 175
1   **6** ones
    + 5 ones
    1 ten, 1 one
	¹¹
	796
	+ 175
	71 **1** ten
	   9 tens
	   + 7 tens
	   1 hundred, 7 tens
		¹
		796
		+ 175
		971 **1** hundred
		   7 hundreds
		   + 1 hundred
		   9 hundreds

Study the example above. Then, solve each problem.

1.

```
    41        324        673         82
  + 26      + 452      + 491      + 471
```

2.

```
   518        793        437        530
 + 276      + 189      + 825      + 986
```

3.

```
   351      1,892      3,576      7,145
 + 1,768    + 2,751    +  763     + 9,374
```

4.

```
 4,592      3,572      2,801      4,921
 + 7,009    + 6,490    + 7,955    + 3,038
```

5.

```
 28,465     65,378     18,647      7,304
 + 37,879   + 43,640   + 23,755    55,47
```

Solving Addition Equations

An **algebraic equation** contains numbers, variables, operations, and an equal sign. In the equation $x + 3 = 10$, x is the **variable** and $+$ is the **operation.** This equation means that an unknown number (called x) plus **3** is equal to **10**. Remember that a variable is a letter that stands for an unknown number.

Solve: $t + 6 = 9$

1. Think: What number plus 6 is equal to 9? $t + 6 = 9$
2. Choose the inverse operation: $t = 9 - 6$ Subtraction is the **inverse** of addition.
   Subtract 6 from each side of the equation. $t = 3$
3. Simplify.
4. Check your solution. $3 + 6 = 9$ The equation is true, so the solution is correct.
   Substitute 3 for t to see if the equation is true. $9 = 9$

Study the example above. Then, solve each equation.

1. $x + 8 = 12$ $\qquad$ $7 + a = 18$ $\qquad$ $z + 6 = 14$
$\quad$ $x = 12 - \underline{\quad}$ $\qquad$ $a = 18 - \underline{\quad}$ $\qquad$ $z = 14 - \underline{\quad}$
$\quad$ $x = \underline{\quad}$ $\qquad$ $a = \underline{\quad}$ $\qquad$ $z = \underline{\quad}$

2. $7 + j = 15$ $\qquad$ $k + 5 = 20$ $\qquad$ $7 + p = 16$
$\quad$ $j = 15 - \underline{\quad}$ $\qquad$ $k = 20 - \underline{\quad}$ $\qquad$ $p = 16 - \underline{\quad}$
$\quad$ $j = \underline{\quad}$ $\qquad$ $k = \underline{\quad}$ $\qquad$ $p = \underline{\quad}$

Solve each equation.

3. $y + 8 = 11$ $\qquad$ $x + 8 = 24$ $\qquad$ $v + 3 = 13$ $\qquad$ $m + 12 = 18$
$\quad$ $y = \underline{\quad}$ $\qquad$ $x = \underline{\quad}$ $\qquad$ $v = \underline{\quad}$ $\qquad$ $m = \underline{\quad}$

4. $c + 7 = 13$ $\qquad$ $n + 6 = 18$ $\qquad$ $h + 9 = 27$ $\qquad$ $s + 16 = 32$
$\quad$ $c = \underline{\quad}$ $\qquad$ $n = \underline{\quad}$ $\qquad$ $h = \underline{\quad}$ $\qquad$ $s = \underline{\quad}$

5. $a + 7 = 20$ $\qquad$ $8 + w = 17$ $\qquad$ $g + 15 = 31$ $\qquad$ $8 + p = 26$
$\quad$ $a = \underline{\quad}$ $\qquad$ $w = \underline{\quad}$ $\qquad$ $g = \underline{\quad}$ $\qquad$ $p = \underline{\quad}$

Subtraction With and Without Regrouping

1. Regroup as needed. Subtract the **ones** column.	2. Regroup as needed. Subtract the **tens** column.	3. Subtract the **hundreds** column.
$\begin{array}{r} {}^{4\ 18} \\ 35\!\!\!/8 \\ -\ 189 \\ \hline 9 \end{array}$ 5 tens as 4 tens, 10 ones	$\begin{array}{r} {}^{2\ 14\ 18} \\ 35\!\!\!/8 \\ -\ 189 \\ \hline 69 \end{array}$ 3 hundreds as 2 hundreds, 10 tens	$\begin{array}{r} {}^{2\ 14\ 18} \\ 35\!\!\!/8 \\ -\ 189 \\ \hline 169 \end{array}$
Remember: 18 ones is the same as 1 ten, 8 ones.		

Study the example above. Then, solve each problem.

1.

$\begin{array}{r} 285 \\ -\ 162 \\ \hline \end{array}$
$\begin{array}{r} 478 \\ -\ 256 \\ \hline \end{array}$
$\begin{array}{r} 871 \\ -\ 557 \\ \hline \end{array}$
$\begin{array}{r} 119 \\ -\ 54 \\ \hline \end{array}$
$\begin{array}{r} 663 \\ -\ 49 \\ \hline \end{array}$

2.

$\begin{array}{r} 852 \\ -\ 451 \\ \hline \end{array}$
$\begin{array}{r} 579 \\ -\ 498 \\ \hline \end{array}$
$\begin{array}{r} 265 \\ -\ 77 \\ \hline \end{array}$
$\begin{array}{r} 565 \\ -\ 178 \\ \hline \end{array}$
$\begin{array}{r} 726 \\ -\ 329 \\ \hline \end{array}$

3.

$\begin{array}{r} 7,462 \\ -\ 189 \\ \hline \end{array}$
$\begin{array}{r} 6,295 \\ -\ 2,174 \\ \hline \end{array}$
$\begin{array}{r} 7,221 \\ -\ 5,321 \\ \hline \end{array}$
$\begin{array}{r} 3,936 \\ -\ 2,878 \\ \hline \end{array}$
$\begin{array}{r} 1,111 \\ -\ 674 \\ \hline \end{array}$

4.

$\begin{array}{r} 9,311 \\ -\ 781 \\ \hline \end{array}$
$\begin{array}{r} 5,322 \\ -\ 693 \\ \hline \end{array}$
$\begin{array}{r} 9,435 \\ -\ 1,634 \\ \hline \end{array}$
$\begin{array}{r} 4,254 \\ -\ 2,965 \\ \hline \end{array}$
$\begin{array}{r} 2,414 \\ -\ 923 \\ \hline \end{array}$

Solving Subtraction Equations

Solve: $y - 8 = 9$

1. Think:
   What number minus 8 is equal to 9? $y - 8 = 9$
2. Choose the inverse operation: $y = 9 + 8$ Addition is the
   Add 8 to each side of the equation. $y = 17$ inverse of
3. Simplify.   subtraction.
4. Check your solution. $17 - 8 = 9$ The equation
   Substitute 17 for y to see if the   is true, so the
   equation is true. $9 = 9$ solution is correct.

Study the example above. Then, solve each equation.

1. $x - 6 = 5$ $n - 8 = 7$ $y - 8 = 13$
   $x = 5 +$ _____ $n = 7 +$ _____ $y = 13 +$ _____
   $x =$ _____ $n =$ _____ $y =$ _____

2. $h - 25 = 17$ $k - 62 = 125$ $100 = p - 20$
   $h = 17 +$ _____ $k = 125 +$ _____ $100 +$ _____ $= p$
   $h =$ _____ $k =$ _____   _____ $= p$

Solve each equation.

3. $g - 19 = 37$ $x - 9 = 27$ $j - 10 = 16$ $m - 8 = 20$
   $g =$ _____ $x =$ _____ $j =$ _____ $m =$ _____

4. $q - 15 = 100$ $r - 19 = 37$ $w - 32 = 32$ $z - 12 = 29$
   $q =$ _____ $r =$ _____ $w =$ _____ $z =$ _____

5. $y - 122 = 45$ $h - 25 = 0$ $a - 16 = 20$ $c - 83 = 24$
   $y =$ _____ $h =$ _____ $a =$ _____ $c =$ _____

Figures of Speech

An **idiom** is a figure of speech. An **idiomatic phrase** has a different meaning than the literal meaning of the individual words.

Fill in the circle next to the best meaning for the boldfaced idiom.

1. Father asked Yasmin to be quiet while he was on the phone. Wayne was intentionally bothering Yasmin. Mother told Yasmin to ignore Wayne or she would **play right into his hands.**
   A. put his hands on her shoulders
   B. fall into a trap that someone plans for ulterior motives
   C. make noise by playing hand instruments

2. While Wendy was reading her novel, she **ran across** the date when World War II began.
   A. moved quickly across a library
   B. crossed out the dates
   C. happened to find information

3. Adrian thought that he was too old to help with the scavenger hunt. Melinda told him to **let his hair down** and join in the fun.
   A. take his hair out of the rubber band
   B. relax
   C. get his hands out of his hair

4. We could hardly **keep a straight face** when Maddie looked at her four-year-old friend and very seriously said, "I believe that you should act your age."
   A. not laugh or smile
   B. not have any curves or angles
   C. keep the drawing of a face as straight as a ruler

5. Brett did not tell Chelsea the secret, because he did not want her to **let the cat out of the bag.**
   A. tell the secret
   B. let the kitten (who was a secret) out of his backpack
   C. rip a hole in the tote bag

Idioms

Use the clues to unscramble the idioms. Write the idioms on the lines.

1. If someone gives you a bike, don't complain that the back tire is flat.
gift mouth look the horse in don't a

_____

2. If you use your brother's old binder instead of buying a new one, you can save enough money for a computer game faster.
is penny penny a saved a earned

_____

3. If you fail the test by just one point, you have still failed the test.
a good mile as as miss is a

_____

4. If your best friend loses a CD that you loaned her, you shouldn't let it ruin your friendship.
make out molehill don't a of mountain a

_____

5. The first grader next door spent his birthday money on candy. He ate it all in one night and became sick.
parted money and a soon his are fool

_____

Extra! Dare to dream! Unscramble the following saying.

hchit ruyo ngawo ot a rtsa

__ __ __ __ __   __ __ __ __ __   __ __ __ __ __

__ __   __ __   __ __ __ __ __.

Opinion Papers

Iesha and her classmates each wrote an opinion paper on the sun. They were required to refer to information studied about the sun and take a position on whether the sun is good, and defend that position. Iesha and Jackie made a Venn diagram based on their papers. Use the information from the diagram to answer the questions (page 33).

causes sunburn

melts ice

causes floods by melting ice and snow

is a star

gives people jobs

tans people's skin

causes aurora borealis

causes skin cancer through overexposure

is the center of our solar system (Earth revolves around it.)

provides warmth for enjoying the beach

makes it too hot in summer

is a clean energy source (solar energy)

makes it too hot and dry in deserts

ejects solar winds

activates plant chlorophyll

is not in many places enough to make solar energy worthwhile

affects weather

dries up mud

usage of fossil fuels

makes people happy

dries out lawns and gardens

inspires people to eat ice cream

causes damage during droughts

inspires artists

Iesha

Jackie

32

Opinion Papers

Read the following statements. Whose paper is more likely to contain each one? Write *Iesha*, *Jackie*, or *both* on the line next to the statement.

_____ **1.** The sun withers millions of acres of farmland each year.

_____ **2.** Although solar energy may help those in sunny climates, those who live in the north find it worthless. Some communities see the sun fewer than three months each year.

_____ **3.** If there were no sun, going to the beach would not be fun. This star at the center of our solar system provides the warmth needed for this excursion.

_____ **4.** The sun has inspired artists throughout the ages. Any art museum provides proof.

_____ **5.** The aurora borealis, or northern lights, is an incredible display of waving colors thanks to solar winds.

_____ **6.** This joy-inspiring star provides a guide for its revolving planets.

_____ **7.** The planets that revolve around the sun burn or freeze depending on how far they are away from it. The only one in exactly the right position to sustain human life is Earth.

Choose a topic from each student's part of the Venn diagram. Highlight the topics. Then, write a sentence or two about the topic using the voice and opinion of that student.

Iesha: _____

_____

_____

Jackie: _____

_____

_____

Multiplication Properties

The zero property: When you multiply a factor by 0, the product is always 0. **8 x 0 = 0**

The identity property (property of one): When you multiply a factor by 1, the product is always the value of that factor. **9 x 1 = 9**

The commutative property: Changing the order of the factors does not change the product. **4 x 5 = 20   5 x 4 = 20**

The associative property: Changing the grouping of factors does not change the product. **(4 x 3) x 2 = 24   4 x (3 x 2) = 24**

The distributive property: A factor multiplied by 2 addends is equal to the sum of each addend individually multiplied by that factor. **8 x (2 + 5) = (8 x 2) + (8 x 5)**

Study the multiplication properties above. Then, complete each equation. Identify the property it shows.

1. 18 x 0 = ___

_____

2. 6 x (3 x 4) = (___ x ___) x ___

_____

3. 8 x 7 = ___ x ___

_____

4. 6 x 12 = 12 x ___

_____

5. (6 x 7) x 4 = 6 x (___ x ___)

_____

6. 12 x ___ = 0

_____

7. 32 x ___ = 32

_____

8. (5 x 6) x 9 = ___ x (6 x ___)

_____

9. 241 x 1 = ___

_____

10. 9 x (4 + 3) = (___ x ___) + (___ x ___)   _____

11. 3 x (12 + 10) = (___ x ___) + (___ x ___)   _____

Solving Multiplication Equations

To solve addition and subtraction equations, use inverse operations. To solve multiplication equations, also use inverse operations. **Inverse operations** are opposites. The inverse of multiplying by a non zero number is dividing by that number.

Solve: $6 \cdot y = 54$

When working with equations, $\cdot$ is often used as a symbol for "multiply."

1. Think:
   What number times 6 is equal to 54?
2. Choose the inverse operation:
   Divide each side of the equation by 6.
3. Simplify.
4. Check your solution. Substitute 9 for y to see if the equation is true.

$y \cdot 6 = 54$ Division is
$y = 54 \div 6$ the inverse of
$y = 9$ multiplication.

$6 \cdot 9 = 54$ The equation
$54 = 54$ is true, so the solution is correct.

Study the example above. Then, solve each equation.

1. $t \cdot 8 = 72$ $n \cdot 9 = 81$ $y \cdot 6 = 42$
   $t = 72 \div$ ____ $n = 81 \div$ ____ $y = 42 \div$ ____
   $t =$ ____ $n =$ ____ $y =$ ____

2. $z \cdot 7 = 35$ $h \cdot 5 = 50$ $k \cdot 7 = 56$
   $z = 35 \div$ ____ $h = 50 \div$ ____ $k = 56 \div$ ____
   $z =$ ____ $h =$ ____ $k =$ ____

Solve each equation.

3. $x \cdot 3 = 12$ $v \cdot 6 = 24$ $h \cdot 8 = 64$ $g \cdot 9 = 27$
   $x =$ ____ $v =$ ____ $h =$ ____ $g =$ ____

4. $n \cdot 6 = 48$ $j \cdot 7 = 14$ $t \cdot 5 = 25$ $d \cdot 4 = 40$
   $n =$ ____ $j =$ ____ $t =$ ____ $d =$ ____

5. $b \cdot 7 = 28$ $f \cdot 3 = 51$ $c \cdot 3 = 36$ $r \cdot 2 = 26$
   $b =$ ____ $f =$ ____ $c =$ ____ $r =$ ____

Dividing by a 1-Digit Number

Divide. 3)1,585	2. Divide the hundreds.	3. Bring down the 8 tens.	4. Bring down the 5 ones.
1. There are not enough thousands to divide. Decide where to place the first digit. Think: 3)15 The first digit of the quotient will be in the hundreds place.	→ **5** 3)1,585 −1 5 0 Multiply 5 x 3. Subtract 15 − 15. Compare 0 < 3.	Think: 3)8 **52** 3)1,585 −1 5 08 Multiply 2 x 3. − 6 Subtract 8 − 6. 2 Compare 2 < 3.	Think: 3)25 **528 r1** 3)1,585 −1 5 08 − 6 25 Multiply 8 x 3. − 24 Subtract 25 − 24. 1 Compare 1 < 3.

Check your answer. Multiply the quotient by the divisor. Add the remainder to the product. The result should be the dividend.

528 ——→ quotient
x   3 ——→ divisor
1,584
+   1 ——→ remainder
1,585 ——→ dividend

Study the example above. Then, solve each problem. Check your answers.

1. 2)1,734   6)2,532   6)674   5)569

2. 7)1,481   6)1,624   5)4;566   4)2,050

3. 8)2,495   7)4,985   4)2,601   3)643

Solving Division Equations

Solve: $n/8 = 9$

1. Think: What number divided by 8 is equal to 9?
2. Choose the inverse operation: Multiply both sides of the equation by 8.
3. Simplify.
4. Check your solution. Substitute 9 for n to see if the equation is true.

The fraction bar is also a division bar: $n/8$ is the same as $n \div 8$.

$n/8 = 9$

$n = 9 \cdot 8$
$n = 72$

Multiplication is the inverse of division.

$72 \div 8 = 9$

$9 = 9$

The equation is true, so the solution is correct.

Study the example above. Then, solve each equation.

1. $x/9 = 4$
   $x = 4 \cdot$ ___
   $x =$ ___

   $f \div 8 = 7$
   $f = 7 \cdot$ ___
   $f =$ ___

   $y/4 = 16$
   $y = 16 \cdot$ ___
   $y =$ ___

2. $v \div 18 = 25$
   $v = 25 \cdot$ ___
   $v =$ ___

   $n/16 = 24$
   $n = 24 \cdot$ ___
   $n =$ ___

   $k \div 12 = 15$
   $k = 15 \cdot$ ___
   $k =$ ___

Solve each equation.

3. $b \div 7 = 7$
   $b =$ ___

   $p \div 6 = 4$
   $p =$ ___

   $t \div 9 = 7$
   $t =$ ___

   $j \div 7 = 6$
   $j =$ ___

4. $c/5 = 10$
   $c =$ ___

   $g \div 4 = 9$
   $g =$ ___

   $y/25 = 75$
   $y =$ ___

   $s \div 22 = 11$
   $s =$ ___

5. $w/9 = 102$
   $w =$ ___

   $k/30 = 18$
   $k =$ ___

   $d/82 = 6$
   $d =$ ___

   $z/29 = 16$
   $z =$ ___

Check Your Summary

A **summary** provides a snapshot of a passage. It should include only details that support the main idea.

Read the summaries. Circle the main idea of each summary. Then, underline the detail that does not support the main idea.

1. Household measuring tools are found in a variety of places. Thermometers are found in water heaters, ovens, and microwaves. Carpets help keep your feet warm. Measuring cups and spoons are in nearly every kitchen. Clocks can be found in bedrooms, kitchens, and bathrooms.

2. Rain forest plants are the topic of the article that I read. Rain forests have animals, like monkeys and sloths. Numerous flowering plants and vines grow on the forest floor. Many of the trees grow to the heights of city buildings. Bromeliads are plants that grow in the canopy of the rain forest.

3. Computers have many uses. They are used to access the Internet. Their word processing programs are used for reports, letters, and schoolwork. They are also used for recreational and educational computer games. Computers even come in many different colors.

4. People believe in many different superstitions. Some people are fearful of numbers, like 13. Others believe in lucky tokens like rabbits' feet. Many people think that superstitions are silly. Some people are certain that you will have seven years of bad luck if you break a mirror.

5. People react differently to anesthesia. Crying uncontrollably is one reaction. Some people become sleepy for several hours after surgery. Anesthesia makes surgery easy for people because they don't experience any pain. Another reaction is becoming temperamental.

6. Limited television-viewing time is important for students and families. It helps students learn by providing more study time. Watching educational television is better than watching horror shows. Less television viewing allows children to have more time to exercise and play. It also gives families more time to interact.

Summary Focus

A **summary focus statement** is a single sentence that describes the topic of a story.

Read the textual details for each summary. Then, circle the best summary focus statement.

1. First, it costs almost a cent to make a cent. Counting and adding pennies takes up a lot of time. Many people do not like having pennies take up space in their pockets, wallets, and purses.

   A. This article tells that the government makes about 14 billion pennies each year.

   B. This article explains many reasons why people think that cents do not make sense.

   C. This article outlines the history of the penny.

2. Banff National Park is located in Alberta, Canada. It is Canada's oldest national park. Quebec, Canada, is home to the Mingan Archipelago National Park Reserve. The archipelago is made up of 40 limestone islands and more than 1,000 granite reefs and islets. Kluane National Park and Reserve in Yukon, Canada, is home to Mount Logan, Canada's highest peak.

   A. The brochure describes and gives the locations of many Canadian national parks.

   B. The brochure describes Canada's historic sites.

   C. The brochure describes Canada's 10 provinces and 3 territories.

3. Salvador Dalí was a famous Spanish artist. He was born in 1904 and lived until 1989. Dalí, one of the greatest artists of the 20th century, was a surrealist painter who found fantasy to be an inspiration.

   A. This book is about surrealist painters.

   B. This anthology of biographies is about painters of the 1900s.

   C. This biography is about Salvador Dalí.

Bamboo

Read the passage.

When bamboo comes to mind, so do images of pandas and China. While this plant is well known for its role in the life cycle of China's endangered pandas, it is now becoming known for its own deterioration. Deforestation is threatening the habitats of as many as half of the world's species of bamboo.

Bamboo has many interesting characteristics. Bamboo is a woody plant, but it is not a tree. It belongs to the grass family. It is the fastest-growing plant on this planet. One species can grow up to four feet in 24 hours. It grows more than 30% faster than the fastest-growing tree. There are more than 1,200 species of bamboo. They are divided by their rhizome, or root, structures into two main types. Sympodial bamboos have clumps of roots and are commonly called *clumpers*; monopodial bamboos have roots that are runners and are commonly called *runners*. Clumpers tend to grow in tropical climates, while runners grow in temperate climates.

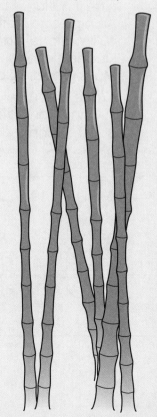

These fast-growing plants share a unique characteristic: they rarely bloom. Each species blooms only once every 7 to 120 years, not every year like most plants. Most bamboo of the same species bloom at approximately the same time. Usually, the parent plant dies soon after flowering.

Bamboo is delicate when it emerges from the ground, but it soon becomes one of the most hardy plants around. The plant craves water when it is first planted, but within a year, it can be somewhat drought tolerant. It tolerates precipitation extremes from 30 to 250 inches of rainfall per year.

Bamboo has many uses. It grows fast, with some types reaching a mature height in just two months. India, China, and Burma have found that a grove of bamboo can be harvested and make a profit in as little as 3 to 5 years. This is much better than rattan, which takes 8 to 10 years to make a profit.

Bamboo

Bamboo is an excellent building material. It is pliable and one of the strongest building materials. In fact, its tensile strength is greater than steel's. Tensile strength refers to how well a material resists breaking under pressure. Steel has a tensile strength of 23,000 psi, while bamboo's tensile strength is a superior 28,000 psi. Bamboo is also an excellent structural material for buildings in earthquake-prone areas. In fact, after the violent 1992 earthquake in Limón, Costa Rica, only the National Bamboo Project's bamboo houses were left standing.

The history of electric lights started with bamboo. Thomas Edison used bamboo during his first experiment with the lightbulb. He used a piece of carbonized bamboo for the filament, or the part that glows to make light. It worked, and light was produced.

Soil conservation is another use of bamboo. Because it grows and matures quickly, it can be planted in deforested areas that have trouble with erosion. Its dense root systems hold the soil in place. Bamboo can also be used to strengthen areas of land that are prone to mud slides and earthquakes.

Bamboo is used to make many items that we use daily. Bamboo pulp is used to make paper. It is also used to make paneling, floor tiles, briquettes for fuel, and rebar to reinforce concrete beams. An antioxidant in pulverized bamboo bark helps prevent the growth of bacteria and is commonly used as a natural food preservative, especially in Japan.

Pandas need bamboo; it may be essential to their survival. Bamboo needs each of us. When we learn to use it to its full potential, we will no longer have to watch it deteriorate or fear that it will become endangered.

Write a summary of the passage. Continue on another sheet of paper, if necessary. Craft your summary statement so that each detail sentence fits the focus.

_____

_____

_____

Greatest Common Factors

The **greatest common factor (GCF)** is the largest factor that can divide 2 or more numbers.

Example: List the factors of 12 and 18. List the common factors. Write the **greatest common factor (GCF).**

Factors of 12: 1, 2, 3, 4, 6, 12
Factors of 18: 1, 2, 3, 6, 9, 18
Common Factors: 1, 2, 3, 6
GCF = 6

Study the example above. Then, list the factors of each number. Circle the common factors for each pair. Find the greatest common factor.

1. 6: _____   4: _____
18: _____   12: _____
GCF: _____   GCF: _____

2. 12: _____   14: _____
18: _____   21: _____
GCF: _____   GCF: _____

3. 18: _____   24: _____
27: _____   32: _____
GCF: _____   GCF: _____

4. 9: _____   9: _____
12: _____   15: _____
GCF: _____   GCF: _____

5. 15: _____   15: _____
20: _____   40: _____
GCF: _____   GCF: _____

6. 14: _____   15: _____
35: _____   35: _____
GCF: _____   GCF: _____

Least Common Multiples

The **least common multiple (LCM)** is the smallest number that is a multiple of two or more numbers.

Example: Find the LCM of 6 and 8.
- List some multiples of 6 and 8.
- List the common multiples.
- Write the least common multiple (LCM).

Multiples of 6:
  6, 12, 18, 24, 30, 36, 42, 48 . . .
Multiples of 8:
  8, 16, 24, 32, 40, 48 . . .
Common Multiples: 24, 48
LCM = 24

Study the example above. Then, find the least common multiple (LCM) for each pair of numbers.

1. 6:_____   4:_____
2:_____   8:_____
LCM:_____   LCM:_____

2. 5:_____   4:_____
3:_____   6:_____
LCM:_____   LCM:_____

3. 8:_____   6:_____
12:_____   10:_____
LCM:_____   LCM:_____

Find the least common multiple (LCM) for each set of numbers.

4. 6:_____   4:_____
5:_____   9:_____
15:_____   18:_____
LCM:_____   LCM:_____

5. 8:_____   10:_____
10:_____   15:_____
20:_____   30:_____
LCM:_____   LCM:_____

Least Common Denominators

Two fractions have a common denominator if their denominators are the same. The **least common denominator (LCD)** of two fractions is the least common multiple of their denominators.

$\frac{5}{8}$ and $\frac{7}{12}$

1. Find the LCM of the two denominators.

Multiples of 8: 8, 16, 24,
Multiples of 12: 12, 24,
Common Multiples: 24
LCM = 24

2. Write equivalent fractions with the common denominator of 24.

$\frac{5}{8} = \frac{}{24}$

$\frac{5}{8} = \frac{5 \times 3}{8 \times 3} = \frac{15}{24}$

$\frac{7}{12} = \frac{}{24}$

$\frac{7}{12} = \frac{7 \times 2}{12 \times 2} = \frac{14}{24}$

Study the example above. Then, rewrite each pair of fractions using their LCD.

1. $\frac{1}{9}$ and $\frac{1}{3}$ $\frac{1}{3}$ and $\frac{1}{6}$ $\frac{5}{6}$ and $\frac{2}{5}$

___ and ___   ___ and ___   ___ and ___

2. $\frac{4}{8}$ and $\frac{2}{3}$ $\frac{2}{6}$ and $\frac{3}{9}$ $\frac{4}{5}$ and $\frac{3}{9}$

___ and ___   ___ and ___   ___ and ___

3. $\frac{2}{4}$ and $\frac{3}{7}$ $\frac{2}{3}$ and $\frac{6}{8}$ $\frac{3}{5}$ and $\frac{5}{6}$

___ and ___   ___ and ___   ___ and ___

Comparing and Ordering

To compare fractions, the fractions must have common denominators.

Example: Compare $\frac{5}{7}$ and $\frac{7}{9}$.

1. Find the LCD.	2. Write equivalent fractions with the LCD.	3. Compare the numerators.
Multiples of 7: 7, 14, 21, 28, 35, 42, 49, 56, 63	$\frac{5}{7} = \frac{}{63}$	$\frac{45}{63} < \frac{49}{63}$
Multiples of 9: 9, 18, 27, 36, 45, 54, 63	$\frac{5}{7} = \frac{5 \times 9}{7 \times 9} = \frac{45}{63}$	So $\frac{5}{7} < \frac{7}{9}$.
Common Multiples: 63	$\frac{7}{9} = \frac{}{63}$	
LCD = 63	$\frac{7}{9} = \frac{7 \times 7}{9 \times 7} = \frac{49}{63}$	

Study the example above. Then, compare each set of fractions using >, <, or = .

1. $\frac{3}{6} \bigcirc \frac{4}{8}$ $\frac{4}{5} \bigcirc \frac{10}{15}$ $\frac{3}{5} \bigcirc \frac{1}{2}$ $\frac{2}{7} \bigcirc \frac{1}{3}$

2. $\frac{2}{3} \bigcirc \frac{5}{8}$ $\frac{1}{3} \bigcirc \frac{2}{5}$ $\frac{1}{8} \bigcirc \frac{1}{16}$ $\frac{5}{9} \bigcirc \frac{4}{8}$

3. $\frac{3}{5} \bigcirc \frac{2}{3}$ $\frac{7}{10} \bigcirc \frac{2}{3}$ $\frac{5}{8} \bigcirc \frac{10}{16}$ $\frac{2}{9} \bigcirc \frac{1}{3}$

Order each set of fractions from least to greatest.

4. $\frac{1}{3}, \frac{7}{12}, \frac{5}{6}, \frac{3}{4}$ _____

5. $\frac{5}{6}, \frac{3}{4}, \frac{1}{2}, \frac{3}{7}$ _____

45

Applesauce Recipe

Ingredients:

- 10–17 tart, firm cooking apples (Macintosh, Spy, Jonathan, or Granny Smith)
- 2 cups sugar
- 1 teaspoon cinnamon (more or less to taste)
- 1 cup liquid (water, apple juice, or apple cider)

Also needed: a paring knife, a large soup kettle with a cover, a colander, a wooden mallet, a spatula, a large mixing bowl, a spoon or scoop, measuring tools, and jars or plastic containers for storage

Directions:

Rinse apples and cut into quarters. Do not peel. Remove cores. Fill the large soup kettle with the apples. Add sugar, cinnamon, and liquid. Cover and simmer on medium heat until apples are no longer firm. Stir frequently. Add more liquid if the mixture becomes too thick. Remove from heat. Set colander in a large bowl. Fill the colander half full with apple mixture. Roll the wooden mallet through the apple mixture, pressing out the applesauce. Roll firmly until peelings are dry. Remove peelings from mallet and colander before adding more cooked apples. Continue until apple mixture has been mashed. Scoop applesauce into jars or plastic containers. Refrigerate for up to one week or freeze for several months.

Highlight one key word or phrase for each direction in the text. Then, number the directions to put them in the correct sequence.

____ Fill the colander with cooked apples.

____ Simmer the apples until they are mushy.

____ Cut the apples into quarters.

____ Refrigerate the applesauce.

____ Add sugar, cinnamon, and liquid.

____ Use water to clean the apples.

____ Place the apples in a pot.

____ Remove the cores.

Doggone Tired

Read the passage.

Kelly and Taffy are dogs. Their favorite place is the backyard. From the top of a hill in the middle of the backyard, they can see almost the entire neighborhood.

One day, Kelly dug a tunnel under the backyard fence. Taffy saw Kelly go under the fence and followed her out of the backyard. They ran as fast as they could down the street, chasing each other and barking. They saw the mail carrier and barked at him as they ran past. Taffy saw a squirrel and chased it up a tall oak tree. Kelly followed, but she was tired of running and sat down under the tree. Taffy was panting from all of the running and barking, so she sat down, too.

Kelly started walking back, trying to find the hole in the fence. Taffy followed. They looked at many fences, but none had a hole under it.

Thirsty and tired, they sat down under a tree beside the road. The mail carrier drove past and saw them. He stopped his truck and walked over to them.

"Ah ha," he said. "Got yourselves lost, did you?" He picked them up and took them home in the mail truck. He led them to the yard and put a big rock in the hole under the fence. Kelly and Taffy ran straight to their water bowl.

Number the events listed to put them in the correct sequence.

_____ Kelly and Taffy ride on the mail truck.

_____ The dogs become thirsty and tired.

_____ Kelly digs a tunnel under the backyard fence.

_____ Taffy chases a squirrel up an oak tree.

_____ The mail carrier speaks to the dogs.

_____ The mail carrier puts a big rock in the hole under the fence.

_____ Taffy follows Kelly out of the backyard.

Find a Penny

Read the passage.

Ben was walking to school with some friends. They saw a bright, shiny penny on the sidewalk. Ben stepped on it.

"Hey," said Mia. "Aren't you going to pick it up?"

"Right," said Ben sarcastically. "'Find a penny; pick it up. Then, all day long you'll have good luck.' If it were a quarter, maybe . . ." He kicked the penny toward the sewer grate and they continued on their way.

They heard the first bell as they rounded the corner to the school. On the way up the steps, Ben tripped and fell, and his backpack went flying. He limped down the hallway after Amber, Trey, and Paige. The last bell rang as Ben hit the door. "Tardy, Ben," said Ms. Davis. "One more and you will have an extra assignment." The classroom phone rang. As Ms. Davis turned her back to the doorway to answer it, Erin quietly slipped into the classroom and took her seat. She had narrowly escaped an extra assignment. "Let's begin by handing in our reading assignments," Ms. Davis said as she turned back toward them. Ben pulled out his folder. His assignment was nowhere to be found!

The morning went from bad to worse. During a three-minute math test, Ben's pencil lead fell out. He wrote two answers, and time was called. During science, his tray tipped over. Dirt, water, a plant, and science tools fell to the floor.

At lunch, Erin requested a piece of pepperoni pizza. "Wow, huge slice!" she said. "Yum! Looks good," thought Ben. He asked for one, too. "Sorry," said Mr. Bentley, "I just served the last one."

Ben flopped into a seat next to Erin. "You sure seem to be having a good day today," he muttered.

Erin laughed, "Yeah, you'll never guess what I picked up next to a sewer grate this morning."

Find a Penny

Answer the following questions about the story (page 48).

1. What kind of day is Ben having? _____

   Highlight specific details in the story that support your answer.

2. What event foreshadows Ben's day? _____

3. What kind of day is Erin having? _____

   Highlight three details in the story that support your answer.

4. What does Erin pick up? _____

5. What do you think Ben will do the next time he sees a penny? ____

   _____

   Explain your answer.

   _____

   _____

   _____

Number the following events to put them in the correct sequence.

____ Ben misses out on pepperoni pizza.

____ Ben's science tray tips over.

____ Erin comes into class late.

____ Ben trips on the school steps.

____ Ben kicks a penny.

____ Erin completes her math facts quiz.

____ Ben cannot find his reading assignment.

Multiplying Fractions

1. Multiply the numerators. Multiply the denominators.	2. Write the fraction in simplest form.
$\dfrac{3}{4} \times \dfrac{2}{8} = \dfrac{3 \times 2}{4 \times 8} = \dfrac{6}{32}$	$\dfrac{6 \div 2}{32 \div 2} = \dfrac{3}{16}$

Study the example above. Then, multiply. Write each fraction in simplest form.

1. $\dfrac{1}{8} \times \dfrac{1}{5} =$ _____ $\qquad$ $\dfrac{1}{4} \times \dfrac{1}{7} =$ _____ $\qquad$ $\dfrac{1}{12} \times \dfrac{1}{8} =$ _____

2. $\dfrac{3}{7} \times \dfrac{4}{5} =$ _____ $\qquad$ $\dfrac{4}{5} \times \dfrac{6}{8} =$ _____ $\qquad$ $\dfrac{2}{3} \times \dfrac{4}{7} =$ _____

3. $\dfrac{5}{6} \times \dfrac{4}{5} =$ _____ $\qquad$ $\dfrac{2}{3} \times \dfrac{7}{8} =$ _____ $\qquad$ $\dfrac{7}{9} \times \dfrac{8}{9} =$ _____

4. $\dfrac{1}{2} \times \dfrac{2}{12} =$ _____ $\qquad$ $\dfrac{2}{3} \times \dfrac{4}{12} =$ _____ $\qquad$ $\dfrac{6}{8} \times \dfrac{4}{16} =$ _____

5. $\dfrac{7}{10} \times \dfrac{3}{5} =$ _____ $\qquad$ $\dfrac{2}{7} \times \dfrac{10}{14} =$ _____ $\qquad$ $\dfrac{4}{6} \times \dfrac{12}{18} =$ _____

6. $\dfrac{12}{16} \times \dfrac{3}{7} =$ _____ $\qquad$ $\dfrac{6}{12} \times \dfrac{5}{6} =$ _____ $\qquad$ $\dfrac{2}{4} \times \dfrac{10}{12} =$ _____

Reciprocals

Two numbers are **reciprocals** of each other when their product is 1.

$\frac{2}{3}$ and $1\frac{1}{2}$ are reciprocals, because $1\frac{1}{2} = \frac{3}{2}$, and $\frac{2}{3} \times \frac{3}{2} = \frac{6}{6}$ or 1.

$1\frac{3}{4}$ and $\frac{4}{7}$ are reciprocals, because $1\frac{3}{4} = \frac{7}{4}$, and $\frac{7}{4} \times \frac{4}{7} = \frac{28}{28}$ or 1.

To find the reciprocal of a fraction, reverse the numerator and the denominator.

Example: Find the reciprocal of $\frac{1}{8}$.

The reciprocal of $\frac{1}{8}$ is $\frac{8}{1}$, or 8.

Find the reciprocal of 15.

- First, write 15 as a fraction. $15 = \frac{15}{1}$

- Then, reverse the numerator and denominator to find the reciprocal. $\frac{1}{15}$

- Check: $\frac{15}{1} \times \frac{1}{15} = \frac{15}{15} = 1$

Find the reciprocal of $4\frac{1}{3}$.

- First, write $4\frac{1}{3}$ as an improper fraction. $4\frac{1}{3} = \frac{13}{3}$

- Then, reverse the numerator and denominator. $\frac{3}{13}$

- Check: $\frac{3}{13} \times \frac{13}{3} = \frac{39}{39} = 1$

Study the examples above. Then, find the reciprocal of each number.

1. $\frac{11}{5} = $ _____ $2\frac{1}{4} = $ _____ $9 = $ _____ $\frac{3}{10} = $ _____ $8\frac{2}{3} = $ _____

2. $\frac{1}{7} = $ _____ $4\frac{5}{8} = $ _____ $\frac{15}{11} = $ _____ $\frac{1}{6} = $ _____ $4\frac{1}{2} = $ _____

3. $\frac{3}{4} = $ _____ $3 = $ _____ $\frac{9}{4} = $ _____ $7\frac{5}{8} = $ _____ $1 = $ _____

4. $5\frac{2}{3} = $ _____ $\frac{7}{9} = $ _____ $27 = $ _____ $2\frac{1}{5} = $ _____ $3\frac{2}{5} = $ _____

Dividing by Fractions

To find $\frac{4}{5} \div \frac{3}{4}$, multiply $\frac{4}{5}$ by the reciprocal of $\frac{3}{4}$.

Reciprocals

Rewrite $\frac{4}{5} \div \frac{3}{4}$ as $\frac{4}{5} \times \frac{4}{3}$.

Then, mulitiply and simplify: $\frac{4 \times 4}{5 \times 3} = \frac{16}{15} = 1\frac{1}{15}$

So, $\frac{4}{5} \div \frac{3}{4} = 1\frac{1}{15}$.

Study the example above. Then, solve each problem.

1.

$\frac{7}{2} \div \frac{1}{2}$

$\frac{7}{2} \times \frac{2}{1} = $ _____

$\frac{4}{3} \div \frac{2}{3}$

$\frac{4}{3} \times \frac{3}{2} = $ _____

$\frac{6}{4} \div \frac{3}{4}$

$\frac{6}{4} \times \frac{4}{3} = $ _____

2.

$\frac{9}{2} \div \frac{1}{3}$

$\frac{9}{2} \times \frac{3}{1} = $ _____

$\frac{8}{3} \div \frac{2}{5}$

$\frac{8}{3} \times \frac{5}{2} = $ _____

$\frac{15}{4} \div \frac{3}{7}$

$\frac{15}{4} \times \frac{7}{3} = $ _____

Divide. Write each answer in simplest form.

3. $\frac{5}{6} \div \frac{5}{9} = $ _____ $\frac{3}{8} \div \frac{3}{4} = $ _____ $\frac{3}{4} \div \frac{5}{2} = $ _____ $\frac{4}{5} \div \frac{4}{3} = $ _____

4. $\frac{5}{8} \div \frac{1}{8} = $ _____ $\frac{4}{7} \div \frac{2}{7} = $ _____ $\frac{5}{8} \div \frac{3}{4} = $ _____ $\frac{2}{5} \div \frac{4}{6} = $ _____

5. $\frac{5}{4} \div \frac{1}{2} = $ _____ $\frac{7}{8} \div \frac{3}{5} = $ _____ $\frac{7}{9} \div \frac{2}{3} = $ _____ $\frac{4}{7} \div \frac{1}{2} = $ _____

Solving Equations with Fractions

1. Rewrite $2\frac{2}{5}$ as an improper fraction.	2. Multiply each side of the equation by the reciprocal of $\frac{5}{12}$, which is $\frac{12}{5}$.	3. Simplify.
$n \times 2\frac{2}{5} = \frac{3}{4}$ $n \times \frac{12}{5} = \frac{3}{4}$	$n \times \frac{12}{5} \times \frac{5}{12} = \frac{3}{4} \times \frac{5}{12}$ $n \times 1 = \frac{3}{4} \times \frac{5}{12}$	$n \times 1 = \frac{3}{4} \times \frac{5}{12}$ $n = \frac{3}{4} \times \frac{5}{12}$ $n = \frac{15}{48}$ $n = \frac{5}{16}$

Study the example above. Then, solve for n.

1. $n \times \frac{3}{4} = \frac{6}{20}$ 　　　　 $n \times \frac{3}{8} = \frac{2}{8}$ 　　　　 $n \times \frac{3}{10} = \frac{2}{3}$

$n =$ _____　　　　　 $n =$ _____　　　　　 $n =$ _____

2. $n \times \frac{1}{2} = \frac{1}{2}$ 　　　　 $n \times \frac{5}{8} = \frac{1}{3}$ 　　　　 $n \times \frac{3}{6} = 1\frac{1}{8}$

$n =$ _____　　　　　 $n =$ _____　　　　　 $n =$ _____

3. $n \times \frac{3}{8} = \frac{1}{8}$ 　　　　 $n \times 1\frac{1}{3} = 3$ 　　　　 $n \times 1\frac{1}{2} = 20$

$n =$ _____　　　　　 $n =$ _____　　　　　 $n =$ _____

4. $n \times 1\frac{1}{2} = 3\frac{1}{2}$ 　　　　 $n \times \frac{1}{8} = \frac{2}{3}$ 　　　　 $n \times \frac{2}{3} = 14$

$n =$ _____　　　　　 $n =$ _____　　　　　 $n =$ _____

5. $n \times \frac{1}{7} = 5\frac{1}{4}$ 　　　　 $n \times \frac{4}{5} = 20$ 　　　　 $n \times 2\frac{3}{4} = 16\frac{1}{2}$

$n =$ _____　　　　　 $n =$ _____　　　　　 $n =$ _____

My New Companion

Read the passage.

I remember the day we met. It was my ninth birthday. My mom and I were pulling into the driveway when I saw it, my new companion. It was awesome! Instantly, I fell in love with the worn, yellow seat and the polished chrome handlebars that gleamed in the afternoon sun. I jumped out of the car and climbed aboard.

It took me a while to feel completely comfortable with my new companion, but before two weeks had passed, we were inseparable. Every day, we would ride, rain or shine. It was on one of those days that we faced our biggest challenge.

My companion and I were cruising along street two blocks from my house when we encountered a group of boys who had set up a ramp. I stopped pedaling and paused to watch as the boys took turns riding their bikes up the ramp.

"Hey there," said a red-headed kid with many freckles as I approached the group, "why don't you give it a try?"

My palms began to sweat, and my heart pounded as I contemplated the possibility that I might crash. Knowing that I would become completely paralyzed with fear if I didn't do something soon, I climbed onto the yellow seat, and let myself go. Without thinking, I started pedaling faster and faster, and before I knew it, I launched into the sky!

It took nearly six weeks for my broken arm to heal. I still went to watch the boys ride their bikes up the ramp. I even made a whole new group of friends, who all signed my cast. The doctor let me keep it as a reminder to be careful.

The minute that I had that cast taken off, I went back to try that jump again. With all of the practice that I've had now, that ramp is no problem. I discovered that whether you're learning to ride a bike, meeting new friends, or taking on a new challenge, overcoming your fear is the first step. Once you do, there's very little that can stop you from achieving your goal!

My New Companion

Answer the following questions using information from the story (page 54).

1. What is the main idea of the story?
- **A.** Learning to ride a bike is fun.
- **B.** It is great to receive presents from parents.
- **C.** It is good to overcome fear.
- **D.** A companion, like a dog, is great.

2. What is a synonym for the word *companion*?
- **A.** bike
- **B.** enemy
- **C.** parent
- **D.** partner

3. Which one of the following statements is an opinion, not a fact?
- **A.** The writer was given a bike for his ninth birthday.
- **B.** Bikes with yellow seats are the best.
- **C.** The writer's companion is a bike.
- **D.** The bike has a worn, yellow seat.

4. Which of the following events happened last?
- **A.** It took nearly six weeks for the writer's broken arm to heal.
- **B.** Instantly, the writer fell in love with the worn, yellow seat and the polished chrome handlebars.
- **C.** The writer's palms began to sweat, and his heart pounded.
- **D.** The writer and his companion were cruising along.

5. What can you infer happened when the boy jumped the ramp for the first time?
- **A.** At the last minute, he was too scared to ride up the ramp.
- **B.** He crashed when he landed.
- **C.** He flew so high that all of the other boys were jealous.
- **D.** He broke his bike when he landed.

Go, Bones!

Read the passage.

Most preteens do not worry about what their bodies will be like when they turn 40 or 50. That seems like such a long way away! Yet, there are some very simple things that can be done before the age of 18 that will have a huge impact on life after 50. It is as simple as exercising, eating right, and getting plenty of calcium and vitamin D, which is needed for calcium absorption.

So, what's the big deal? The problem is osteoporosis—a big word that means bones are losing mass and are more apt to break or fracture. Osteoporosis can even cause collapsed vertebrae, resulting in incredible back pain and spinal deformities, like a rounded back.

Osteoporosis cannot be cured. The best way to take care of it is to prevent it. The best time to prevent osteoporosis is before the age of 18. From birth to the late teens, people build their greatest amount of bone mass.

The problem is that many children are not getting enough calcium in their diets. Milk and other dairy products are rich in calcium. Several studies have shown that girls and boys who drink a lot of soft drinks and fruit beverages tend to drink less milk. Other studies have shown that cola and caffeinated beverages leach calcium out of the bones, which means that more calcium is needed to compensate.

Most adults need about 1000 mg of dietary calcium per day, without drinking cola; children need slightly more. People under 18 years old need the equivalent of four to five glasses of milk each day. For those who don't like milk, the good news is that calcium can also be found in other foods, like yogurt, cheese, green leafy vegetables, and broccoli.

You have the power to take preventative measures now. Armed with knowledge, you can have a direct impact on what your own life will be like many years from now.

Go, Bones!

Answer each of the following questions and underline your answers in the passage (page 56).

1. What is osteoporosis? _____

   _____

2. List two possible consequences of a person having osteoporosis.

   _____

3. Why should kids be concerned about osteoporosis? _____

   _____

   _____

4. When is the most bone mass grown? _____

5. Why is milk important to this issue? _____

6. What can you eat if you do not like to drink milk? _____

7. What effect do caffeinated beverages have on the bones? _____

   _____

8. What, besides calcium, will strengthen your bones and help prevent osteoporosis?

   _____

9. Evaluate your own lifestyle. What can you do to help your bones?

   _____

   _____

   _____

Rounding Decimals

14.6$\underline{5}$3 ⟶ 14.65 (Drop the 3.) $\underline{6}$.79 ⟶ 7 (Drop the .79.)	Look to the right of the underlined place value. If that number is 5 or greater, round up. If not, keep the number the same. Remember to drop all of the numbers to the right of the rounded number.

Study the examples above. Then, round each decimal to the underlined place value.

1. 141.3$\underline{6}$7   39.987   15.3$\underline{1}$5

2. 4.29$\underline{7}$4   0.0$\underline{8}$5   27.7$\underline{9}$1

3. 546.0$\underline{8}$1   3.$\underline{2}$06   13.0$\underline{7}$6

4. 44$\underline{3}$.788   4.0$\underline{9}$8   607.$\underline{8}$3

5. 16.65$\underline{3}$8   67.$\underline{2}$6 $\underline{5}$.568

6. 2.7$\underline{6}$1   5.$\underline{5}$09   6.2$\underline{9}$45

7. 2$\underline{1}$.04   99.$\underline{3}$8   635.68$\underline{1}$5

8. 59.5$\underline{9}$ 1$\underline{7}$.891   53.5$\underline{7}$

9. It takes the moon an average of 27.32167 days to revolve around Earth. Is the length of time closer to 27 or 28 days?

Adding Decimals

Add 152.6 + 0.765.

1. Line up the decimal points. Place a 0 where it helps you add.	2. Add. Write the decimal point in the answer.
152.600 ← Place **0** in the + 0.765 hundredths and thousandths places.	$\overset{1}{1}$52.600 + 0.765 **153.365**

Study the example above. Then, solve each problem.

1.
$$0.9$$
$$+ 0.47$$

$$6$$
$$+ 7.48$$

$$8.043$$
$$+ 3.97$$

$$6.08$$
$$+ 48.463$$

$$37.27$$
$$+ 84.948$$

2.
$$36.764$$
$$+ 877.3$$

$$97.4$$
$$+ 73.969$$

$$53.903$$
$$+ 99.8$$

$$0.6$$
$$+ 69.427$$

$$47.67$$
$$+ 0.4$$

3.
$$0.6$$
$$0.47$$
$$+ 0.22$$

$$24.69$$
$$0.104$$
$$+ 682.62$$

$$7$$
$$32.08$$
$$+ 456.643$$

$$28.1$$
$$7.786$$
$$+ 246.907$$

$$39.48$$
$$12.2$$
$$+ 473.745$$

4.
$$6.107$$
$$65.48$$
$$+ 183$$

$$0.72$$
$$2.1$$
$$+ 135.461$$

$$0.74$$
$$8$$
$$+ 10.9$$

$$0.5$$
$$9.43$$
$$+ 0.002$$

$$4.673$$
$$38.09$$
$$+ 196.4$$

5.   97.483 + 73.99 =   5.903 + 99.1 =   18.7 + 6.427 =

_____   _____   _____

6.   74.36 + 8.758 =   8.05 + 139.5 + 98.004 =   78 + 746.78 + 9.463 =

_____   _____   _____

Multiplying Decimals

Multiply **1.05 x 0.03.**

1. Multiply as you would with whole numbers.

$$\begin{array}{r} \overset{1}{1.05} \\ \times\ \ 0.03 \\ \hline 315 \end{array}$$

2. Add the number of decimal places in the factors. Then, use the sum to place the decimal point in your answer. Write 0 to show extra places.

$$\begin{array}{r} \overset{1}{1.05} \leftarrow 2\text{ decimal places} \\ \times\ \ 0.03 \leftarrow 2\text{ decimal places} \\ \hline 0.0315 \leftarrow 4\text{ decimal places needed in} \end{array}$$

answer, but only 3 numbers

Write 0 as a placeholder.

Study the example above. Then, solve each problem.

1.

0.091	0.0072	0.0043	0.025
x 0.02	x 0.07	x 0.9	x 0.04

2.

0.33	0.14	0.305	0.45
x 0.0053	x 0.0048	x 0.008	x 0.007

3.

0.165	9.7	0.025	0.057
x 0.08	x 0.002	x 0.6	x 0.43

4.

0.092	0.125	0.0047	0.309
x 0.086	x 0.023	x 0.83	x 0.09

5.

0.103	0.017	0.0096	0.031
x 0.005	x 0.17	x 0.37	x 0.022

Dividing Decimals

Divide 0.192 ÷ 32.

$$32\overline{)0.192}$$ ← First, put the decimal point in the quotient directly above the decimal point in the dividend.

Then, divide.

$$
\begin{array}{r}
0.006 \\
32\overline{)0.192} \\
-\ 192 \\
\hline
0
\end{array}
$$

Study the example above. Then, solve each problem.

1. $4\overline{)2.8}$ $7\overline{)0.56}$ $2\overline{)0.018}$ $3\overline{)0.21}$

2. $8\overline{)0.52}$ $8\overline{)0.19}$ $5\overline{)0.451}$ $6\overline{)0.1065}$

3. $24\overline{)0.15}$ $65\overline{)1.95}$ $10\overline{)62.4}$ $29\overline{)0.174}$

4. $31\overline{)0.6417}$ $12\overline{)0.42}$ $27\overline{)94.5}$ $59\overline{)1.947}$

Water around Us

Read the study guide.

- Water is found in three states: solid, liquid, and gas.
  solid: ice (frozen water), glaciers (rivers of ice), icebergs (floating pieces of glaciers), frost (ice crystals on objects)
  liquid: rivers, runoff (flows across land), lakes, oceans, ground water
  gas: water vapor, steam

- Water as a gas is called *water vapor*.

- Water is continually changing states. Each change is a part of the never-ending water cycle: evaporation, condensation, precipitation, and storage (reservoir).

- Evaporation is the change from a liquid state to a gas state. Water on the surface changes to water vapor when the air becomes warmer.

- Three things can help speed up evaporation: heat, wind, and increased surface area.

- Condensation occurs when water changes from a gas back to a liquid.

- In the water cycle, condensation refers to clouds and fog. Clouds form when water vapor rises and cools, condensing on very small particles in the air, like dust. In cold air, the water vapor changes to small ice crystals. Clouds are formed from millions of these drops or crystals.

- Fog is a cloud near the ground.

- Precipitation is water that falls from clouds.
  rain: liquid water that falls when the air is warmer than 0°C (32°F)
  snow: ice crystals that fall when the air is cooler than 0°C (32°F)
  sleet: frozen rain
  hail: small spheres formed from many layers of ice

- Storage, or reservoir, is a place that stores water. Examples include lakes, rivers, ground water, plants, glaciers, pools, water towers, and swamps.

- Most of the liquid water on Earth is salt water.

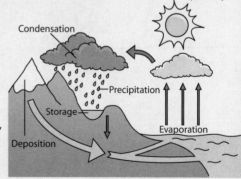

Water around Us

Match the terms with the descriptions. Write the letter on each line.

_____ A place that stores water

_____ It moves through soil and rocks.

_____ It shows how water is always changing states.

_____ Rain, sleet, and snow

_____ How clouds are formed

_____ Changing from liquid water to water vapor

_____ A large tank used as a reservoir

_____ A large river of ice

_____ Water that flows across land

_____ A large block of ice floating in the ocean

> A. evaporation
> B. iceberg
> C. runoff
> D. condensation
> E. reservoir
> F. ground water
> G. water tower
> H. water cycle
> I. precipitation
> J. glacier

Answer the following questions.

1. In what three states can water be found on Earth?

_____ _____ _____

2. Where can liquid water be found on Earth? Give three examples.

_____ _____ _____

3. What kinds of precipitation can be found at these temperatures?

-2°C _____ **15°C** _____

4. List four different uses of water.

_____ _____

_____ _____

5. Is most of the liquid water on Earth fresh water or salt water? _____

6. What three things can help speed up evaporation?

_____ _____ _____

63

Water around Us

Circle the letter next to the answer.

7. Water that falls from clouds is
    A. condensation.   **B.** precipitation.   **C.** evaporation.

8. A cloud very close to the ground is
    A. sleet.   **B.** hail.   **C.** fog.

9. Which of the following does not speed up evaporation?
    A. wind   **B.** decreased surface area **C.** heat

10. Water vapor may condense to liquid water when it
    A. becomes cooler. **B.** becomes warmer. **C.** evaporates.

11. Evaporation takes place where water is
    A. in the air.   **B.** on the surface.   **C.** deep below the surface.

12. Ice crystals that form on objects are called
    A. snow.   **B.** frost.   **C.** sleet.

13. Frozen rain is called
    A. hail.   **B.** sleet.   **C.** clouds.

14. Precipitation that falls as liquid water is
    A. hail.   **B.** sleet.   **C.** rain.

15. Liquid water evaporates when the air
    A. becomes cooler. **B.** becomes warmer. **C.** condenses.

Answer the following questions in complete sentences.

A. What is water vapor? _____

B. How do clouds form? _____

_____

_____

Camping on Frog Pond

Read the two campers' descriptions of waking up at Frog Pond. Then, answer the following questions.

Camper One

We woke this morning to waves lapping the shore, a breeze rustling the leaves, and baby frogs croaking to each other. They woke the swans and ducks, who sang good morning to the animals around the pond. Soon, every insect, bird, and animal was calling good morning to each other. How could I stay in bed? I needed to greet the morning, too.

Camper Two

We woke this morning to the incessant sound of frogs in the pond. Their noisy alarm triggered off-key honking and quacking from around the pond. The waves slapped the shore while the wind sandpapered everything in its path. Within 60 seconds, every insect, bird, and animal seemed to be protesting the hour. With this continuous cacophony, it was hardly worth going back to sleep.

1. How does Camper One feel about waking up at Frog Pond?_____

_____

2. How does Camper Two feel about waking up at Frog Pond? _____

_____

3. After reading both pieces, write four facts about what happened at Frog Pond that morning. Do not include any opinion words.

_____

_____

_____

_____

_____

_____

Plane Figures

A **point** is a location in space. **Space** is the set of all points.
A **plane** is a set of points that forms a flat surface extending in all directions without limit. Here are some figures that are contained in a plane:

Segment	**Ray**	**Line**
The endpoints of this segment are A and B.	A ray has one endpoint and extends forever in the other direction.	The arrows show that a line extends forever in both directions.

A ⎯⎯⎯ B

R   S

C   D

segment AB, or $\overline{AB}$

segment BA, or $\overline{BA}$

ray RS, or $\overrightarrow{RS}$

line CD, or $\overleftrightarrow{CD}$

line DC, or $\overleftrightarrow{DC}$

Study the figures above. Then, write the name or names of each figure shown.

1.

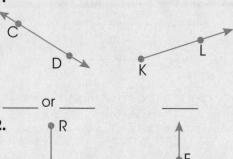

_____ or _____   _____   _____ or _____   _____ or _____

2.

_____ or _____   _____   _____   _____ or ___

Draw an example of each figure.

3.   line XY   segment PQ   ray GH   line YZ

Classifying Lines

If lines cross through the same point, they **intersect.** If they intersect at right angles (90° angles), they are **perpendicular.** If they do not intersect, they are **parallel.**

The lines intersect.

The lines are perpendicular.

The lines are parallel.

Rays and segments can also intersect or be perpendicular or parallel.

Study the examples above. Then, match each description with the correct figure.

1. ____ intersecting rays

2. ____ parallel segments

3. ____ perpendicular line and ray

4. ____ intersecting segment and line

5. ____ perpendicular lines

6. ____ parallel ray and segment

7. ____ parallel line and ray

8. ____ segments intersecting at point P

9. ____ perpendicular segment and ray intersecting at endpoint S

A.

B.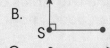

C.

D.

E.

F.

G.

H.

I.

Classifying Lines

Two rays that share a common endpoint form an **angle.** The common endpoint is the **vertex** of the angle. The rays are the **sides** of the angle.

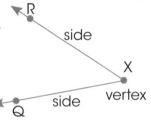

The symbol ∠ represents an angle. When naming an angle, the letter that names the vertex must be in the middle. The angle at the right is ∠**QXR** or ∠**RXQ.**

An **acute angle** is smaller than a right angle.

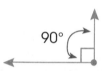

A **right angle** is like the corner of an index card.

An **obtuse angle** is greater than a right angle but not a straight line.

Study the examples above. Then, name each angle. Classify the angle as acute, right, or obtuse.

1.

_____

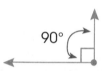

_____

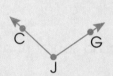

_____

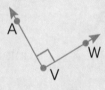

_____

2.

_____

_____

_____

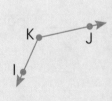

_____

Classifying Angles

Perimeter is the distance around a figure.

7 in.

3 in.

$P = (2 \times 3) + (2 \times 7) = \textbf{20 in.}$

Area is the measure of the space inside a figure.

6 in.

20 in.

$A = b \times h$
$A = 20 \times 6$
$A = \textbf{120 sq. in.}$

Study the examples above. Then, find the perimeter and the area of each quadrilateral.

1. 5 m

5 m

P = _____

A = _____

2. 10 m

4 m

P = _____

A = _____

3. 30 cm

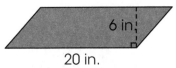 10 cm   12 cm

P = _____

A = _____

4. 6 cm

6 cm

P = _____

A = _____

5.   16 m 18 m

20 m

P = _____

A = _____

6.   4 yd.

20 yd.

P = _____

A = _____

7. 9 ft.

9 ft.

P = _____

A = _____

8. 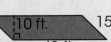 10 ft. 15 ft.

40 ft.

P = _____

A = _____

Babe Didrikson Zaharias

Read the passage.

Mildred Ella "Babe" Didriksen was born in Port Arthur, Texas, in 1911. She said that she received her nickname after hitting five home runs in a baseball game. Some biographers have noted that her mother, a Norwegian immigrant, called her "Min Babe" as a nickname. As an adult, Babe changed the spelling of her last name to make it sound more Norwegian. In 1938, she married a professional wrestler named George Zaharias.

One of the greatest female athletes of all time, Babe competed in sports throughout her life. Women were not allowed to play many sports in her time, so she took every chance she had to play and compete. Babe was voted the Woman Athlete of the First Half of the 20th Century in a poll. She was also named the Woman Athlete of the Year in 1931, 1945, 1946, 1947, 1950, and 1954.

Best known today as a golfer, she knew little about golf growing up in Beaumont, Texas. In fact, she had gained world fame in track and field and All-American status in basketball before she took up golf. She also mastered tennis, played organized baseball and softball, and was an expert diver, roller skater, and bowler. In track and field, she either held or tied the world record in four events—the javelin throw, 80-meter hurdles, high jump, and long jump—and won two gold medals and one silver medal in the 1932 Olympics.

Already famous, Babe began concentrating on golf in 1935 at the suggestion of sportswriter Grantland Rice. For a time, she was not allowed to play in amateur golf tournaments because she was earning too much money playing basketball and baseball. She played in her first golf tournament a year after learning the rules of the game of golf. In 1946 and 1947, she won 17 amateur golf tournaments in a row.

As a professional golfer, she was a founder and a charter member of the Ladies Professional Golf Association (LPGA). She later became a member of the Golf Hall of Fame. Babe always loved playing sports, and she really loved winning. She had to work hard for her accomplishments, but her hard work paid off for her and other women. Today, it is much easier for girls to play any sport that they want to play. Babe, and other women like her, showed the world that women can be professional athletes, too!

Babe Didrikson Zaharias

Answer the following questions about the passage (page 70).

1. What was Babe's favorite thing to do?
   - **A.** play baseball, basketball, and golf
   - **B.** play baseball and basketball
   - **C.** play any sport
   - **D.** play tennis and golf

2. Where was Babe from?
   - **A.** Texas
   - **B.** Oklahoma
   - **C.** Colorado
   - **D.** Mississippi

3. What title did she receive six different years?
   - **A.** Olympic Athlete of the Year
   - **B.** World's Best Female Athlete
   - **C.** Woman Athlete of the Year
   - **D.** Professional Woman Golfer

4. Where did Babe grow up?
   - **A.** Port Arthur, Texas
   - **B.** Austin, Texas
   - **C.** Beaumont, Texas
   - **D.** Dallas, Texas

5. What medals did she receive in the 1932 Olympics?
   - **A.** two gold and one silver
   - **B.** two gold and two silver
   - **C.** three gold and one silver
   - **D.** two gold and no silver

6. Which of the following sports is Babe best known for today?
   - **A.** basketball
   - **B.** golf
   - **C.** tennis
   - **D.** track

7. In your own words, explain how playing sports is different today than it was 60 years ago for female athletes.

   _____

   _____

   _____

   _____

   _____

   _____

Asthma

Read the passage.

You just found out that your friend has asthma. All sorts of scary questions are running through your mind: Can I catch it? Is it safe to be around my friend? Will my friend spend a lot of time indoors or in the hospital?

First, asthma is not contagious. You cannot catch it from someone else. Anyone can develop asthma, including children and adults. There is some evidence that the tendency to develop asthma may be hereditary, or passed on by parents, just like hair color or body size.

What is asthma? Asthma is a chronic condition of two of the body's vital organs. These vital organs are the lungs. Asthma cannot be cured, but it can be managed with medications and by avoiding triggers.

Understanding how the lungs work can help you understand what asthma is. The lungs are made up of bronchi, which are interconnecting passageways that let oxygen and carbon dioxide pass between the body and the outside air. The bronchi branch off into smaller passageways called bronchioles. This entire system is often called the brachial tree. The bronchi are covered with cilia, which are small, hairlike projections that use mucus to sweep dust and other particles out of the lungs.

Asthma is a lung condition that acts differently with different people. However, all asthmatics, or people with asthma, have oversensitive lungs. They have problems when the muscles surrounding the bronchi squeeze too tightly and the brachial tree produces too much mucus. This can make it hard for the asthmatic person to breathe. Because the airways are tighter and contain extra mucus, carbon dioxide gets trapped in the lower parts of the brachial tree, which results in a smaller area of the lungs being used for breathing. When oxygen is brought into the lungs, a smaller part of the lungs is able to absorb it and bring it to the body. The problem is not taking in oxygen: it is releasing the trapped carbon dioxide. The good news is that the lungs do not behave this way all of the time—only when a trigger is present.

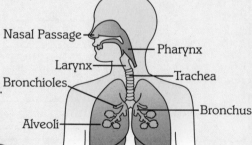

Nasal Passage
Pharynx
Larynx
Bronchioles
Trachea
Bronchus
Alveoli

Asthma

When an asthma attack occurs, a trigger causes the airways to constrict, or get smaller, and produce more mucus, trapping carbon dioxide in the lungs. Triggers are different for each asthmatic and can include allergens, irritants, viruses or bacteria, exercise, or stress. Just because a person has an allergy does not mean he has or will have asthma, just as a person who has asthma does not necessarily have allergies.

Asthmatics can lead normal lives. They can play sports, travel, and do all sorts of fun things. They do, however, need to be aware of their own triggers. Different things trigger asthma in different patients. Knowledge, the correct medications and equipment, and a good working relationship with a doctor are an asthmatic's best tools.

Answer the questions using information from the passage.

1. What does the word *chronic* mean in paragraph 3? _____

   _____

   Highlight the answer in the passage with yellow.

2. What are bronchi? _____

   _____

   Highlight the answer in the passage with green.

3. How do bronchi affect an asthmatic? _____

   _____

4. What is a trigger? _____

   _____

   Highlight the answer in the passage with blue.

5. List four possible triggers.

   _____   _____

   _____   _____

Writing Ratios

A **ratio** compares two quantities and can be written in several different ways.

"3 circles to 4 squares" can be written as:

$\frac{3}{4}$ 3:4   3 to 4

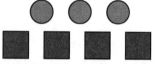

Study the example above. Then, write each ratio three different ways.

1. 4 balls to 6 bats
_____

2. 10 bicycles to 9 helmets
_____

3. 5 bananas to 7 apples
_____

4. 3 comedies to 4 dramas
_____

5. 5 shirts to 4 sweaters
_____

6. 12 peanuts to 18 raisins
_____

7. 6 oranges to 11 bananas
_____

8. 13 peaches to 15 plums
_____

9. 11 girls to 23 students
_____

10. 12 boys to 23 students
_____

11. 1 teacher to 26 students
_____

12. 3 administrators to 950 students
_____

13. 2 giraffes to 5 gorillas
_____

14. 18 flamingos to 9 parrots
_____

15. 3 tigers to 4 lions
_____

16. 7 monkeys to 8 apes
_____

17. The ratio of boys to girls in the school orchestra is 22:25.

Are there more boys or more girls in the orchestra? _____

Equal Ratios

$\frac{3}{4} \bowtie \frac{2}{3}$

$3 \times 3 = 9$
$4 \times 2 = 8$

(no)

To find equal ratios:
1. Cross multiply.
2. If the **cross products** are equal, then the ratios are equal.

$\frac{2}{3} = \frac{x}{12}$

$\frac{2}{3} \times \frac{4}{4} = \frac{8}{12}$

Since $3 \times 4 = 12$, multiply 2×4 to find x.

Study the example above. Then, determine whether each pair of ratios is equal. Write yes or no.

1. $\frac{9}{10}, \frac{8}{9}$ _____ $\frac{14}{16}, \frac{7}{8}$ _____ $\frac{5}{6}, \frac{10}{11}$ _____

2. $\frac{4}{5}, \frac{12}{15}$ _____ $\frac{3}{8}, \frac{6}{16}$ _____ $\frac{6}{9}, \frac{8}{12}$ _____

3. $\frac{6}{5}, \frac{7}{6}$ _____ $\frac{8}{20}, \frac{6}{15}$ _____ $\frac{12}{20}, \frac{6}{15}$ _____

Study the example above. Then, find what x equals.

4. $\frac{15}{20} = \frac{x}{40}$ $\frac{2}{3} = \frac{x}{9}$ $\frac{4}{5} = \frac{x}{15}$

X = _____   X = _____   X = _____

5. $\frac{5}{9} = \frac{x}{27}$ $\frac{75}{100} = \frac{x}{4}$ $\frac{8}{10} = \frac{x}{20}$

X = _____   X = _____   X = _____

6. $\frac{12}{15} = \frac{x}{30}$ $\frac{5}{4} = \frac{x}{12}$ $\frac{24}{30} = \frac{x}{15}$

X = _____   X = _____   X = _____

Understanding Percent

52:100 = 52%

$\frac{75}{100}$ = 75%

A **percent** is a ratio that compares a quantity to 100.

Study the example above. Then, write each ratio as a percent.

1. 29:100 = _____ $\frac{61}{100}$ = _____ $\frac{8}{100}$ = _____   25:100 = _____

2. 5 to 100 = _____   85:100 = _____   97 to 100 = _____ $\frac{67}{100}$ = _____

3. 40 to 100 = _____   13:100 = _____ $\frac{51}{100}$ = _____   75:100 = _____

Write each percent as a ratio (in fraction form). Write each fraction in simplest terms.

4. 50% = _____   30% = _____   25% = _____   20% = _____

5. 73% = _____   64% = _____   15% = _____   40% = _____

6. 60% = _____   33% = _____   75% = _____   10% = _____

7. 63% = _____   95% = _____   70% = _____   86% = _____

8. A theater reviewer wrote that a lead actress "gave 100% effort." What do you think the reviewer meant about the actress's performance?

_____

_____

_____

Finding the Percent of a Number

Fraction Method	Decimal Method
75% of 60	51% of 80
$75\% = \dfrac{75}{100} = \dfrac{3}{4}$	$51\% = \dfrac{51}{100} = 0.51$
$\dfrac{3}{4} \times 60$	0.51×80
45	**40.8**

Study the two methods above. Then, find the percent of each number.

1. 50% of 24   10% of 20   25% of 24

_____   _____   _____

2. 6% of 60   40% of 50   5% of 60

_____   _____   _____

3. 20% of 25   24% of 30   15% of 20

_____   _____   _____

4. 35% of 70   50% of 36   30% of 90

_____   _____   _____

5. 10% of 80   40% of 26   4% of 50

_____   _____   _____

6. 40% of 100   25% of 62   90% of 30

_____   _____   _____

7. 10% of 150   50% of 88   33% of 200

_____   _____   _____

Compare each set of numbers using <, >, or =.

8.   100% of 55 $\bigcirc$ 55   85% of 55 $\bigcirc$ 55   125% of 55 $\bigcirc$ 55

Getting the Setting

The **setting** includes both the time and place.

Identify each setting in the paragraphs. Write the place and circle the time. Highlight the words that helped you find the answers.

1. Heath studied the *Tyrannosaurus rex* display at the Field Museum in Chicago. He filled in several answers on his field trip questionnaire.

   Where? _____

   When?   in the past   in the present   in the future

2. Jill was exhausted. She woke at sunup to cook breakfast over the campfire and help load the wagon. Then, she got in line with the other wagons. Eight hours later, she was still sitting on the buckboard trying to guide the oxen. She hoped that the place called California was worth the three-month trip.

   Where? _____

   When?   in the past   in the present   in the future

3. Kayla flopped on her bed. She couldn't wait to get her gumbawa. It was the best pet in the universe! Her brother Kyle had promised to bring her one. She would be the first person in Idaho to have one. Kyle's hyperspace transport from Uranna Four was due back on Earth this week.

   Where? _____

   When?   in the past   in the present   in the future

4. Tyrone watched the eagle through his binoculars. He was glad that he had the weekend to research his spring project on Oregon eagles. He observed the female eagle return to the nest at the top of the enormous pine with food for the young one.

   Where? _____

   When?   in the past   in the present   in the future

Within Time

A **time frame** is a specific period of time. It tells you when an event happened or when it will take place.

Example:

in the past:	Willow rode the stagecoach to New Mexico.
in the present:	Willow rode in the van to the store.
in the future:	Willow rode the rocket to Jupiter.

Read each sentence to determine the time frame. Write *past, present*, or *future* to show when the action happened. Highlight the word or words that helped you find your answer. Then, rewrite the sentence so that the action happens in the other two time frames. Write *past, present*, or *future* for the rewritten sentences.

1. _____ Jayla used her computer to write the story.

_____ _____

_____ _____

2. _____ Urg paid for the raw dinosaur meat with four rocks.

_____ _____

_____ _____

3. _____ Erin toasted her grilled cheese sandwich on the stove.

_____ _____

_____ _____

4. _____ Paolo loved his virtual reality novel. He could actually smell and feel the terrain of Yerba, Mars.

_____ _____

_____ _____

Milkweed

Read the text and answer the questions.

Maddie stood by the side of the road. She turned over yet another pale green leaf. No caterpillar. In her other hand, covered with sticky, milky fluid, was a nearly empty ice cream bucket. One lone black-, yellow-, and white-striped caterpillar was monotonously eating larger and larger swaths out of the leaf on the milkweed stem that she had placed in there for its lunch. At this rate, she would need more leaves before leaving for school in the morning. Maddie looked up. She saw her friend Jade approaching. Jade parked her bike. "What are you looking for?" she asked.

"I promised my teacher that I would bring five monarch caterpillars for our first science lesson this year. I've found only one so far." Jade put down her kickstand and began to help Maddie. She looked on several milkweed leaves and then moved over to look at the stem of a dandelion.

"Don't look there," said Maddie. "Monarch caterpillars eat only milkweed leaves. I've looked over this patch twice and can't find any more."

"No problem," Jade replied. "There is a huge patch of milkweed behind my house."

1. What is the setting? _____

2. Who are the characters? Circle the name of each character once in the story. _____

3. What is the problem? _____

   _____

4. What is your predicted solution? _____

   _____

   Highlight details in the story that helped you think of a solution.

5. Write two facts about monarch caterpillars. _____

   _____

What's the Problem?

Read the paragraph. Write the problem on the line. Then, pick one of the problems. Write a good solution to the problem on the lines provided.

1. Porchia stared at the massive mess in her room. It had to be clean before she could leave for the movie. "Oh, why didn't I start this on Monday?" she thought. "The movie starts in two hours. I'll never finish in time!"

   Problem: _____

2. "Look at that!" yelled Tom. Rob grabbed his arm and started to run toward the stairs. "We should not have dared him to do it," said Rob. Tony was soaring down the stairs' handrail on his skateboard.

   Problem: _____

3. Darryl wanted to be in the school play. Tryouts were Thursday after school. The bus would be gone by the time tryouts were finished, and neither of Darryl's parents would be able to pick him up.

   Problem: _____

4. Ana grabbed her favorite sweater from the drawer. She started to button it up. Suddenly, a button popped off the sweater and dropped onto the floor with a clunk.

   Problem: _____

5. Eric wanted a new MP3 player. He thought that he would get one for his birthday, but he didn't. He received $40 instead. The MP3 player that he wanted cost $87.

   Problem: _____

6. **Solution:** _____

   _____

   _____

   _____

   _____

   _____

Chance and Probability

Flip a coin. What is the **probability** that it will land on heads? Tails?

P (Heads) $= \dfrac{1}{2}$

P (Tails) $= \dfrac{1}{2}$

Since there are two sides, one heads and one tails, there is a 1 out of 2 ($\dfrac{1}{2}$) chance that it will land on a certain side.

Study the example above. Then, determine the probability of each situation. Express each answer as a fraction in simplest terms.

Roll a die.

1. odd number

2. even number

3. a number less than 3

4. a number greater than 2

5. 3

6. a number less than 7

Pick a card from a standard deck of 52 playing cards.

7. a jack of spades

8. a 4 of hearts

9. a black 11

10. a 6

11. a red card

12. a queen or a king

13. a diamond

14. a red ace

Finding Averages

To find an **average** of a set of numbers: 1. Add the numbers. 2. Divide by the number of addends.	9, 11, 7, 8 9 + 11 + 7 + 8 = 35 35 ÷ 4 = 8.8

Study the example above. Then, find the average of each set of numbers. Round to the nearest tenth.

1. 8, 9, 10

_____

5, 5, 7, 3

_____

5, 4, 9, 10

_____

2. 3, 3, 12, 4, 6

_____

7, 9, 5, 12

_____

4, 9, 13, 5, 11

_____

3. 6, 8, 7, 7, 8

_____

12, 3, 9, 8

_____

9, 11, 8, 12

_____

4. 8, 12, 11, 10

_____

15, 9, 12, 10, 11

_____

7, 6, 9, 7, 8

_____

5. 275, 350, 421

_____

78, 109, 101, 111

_____

65, 99, 87, 67

_____

6. 123, 72, 209

_____

65, 78, 93, 81

_____

67, 87, 103, 99

_____

Mean, Median, and Mode

6, 7, 7, 8, 7, 5

Mean (or average):	Add the numbers and divide by the number of addends. $(6 + 7 + 7 + 8 + 7 + 5) \div 6 = 40 \div 6 = 6.7$ **Mean = 6.7**
Median (middle number):	Arrange the numbers in order. Find the middle number. If there is not one middle number, average the two numbers in the middle. 5, 6, 7, 7, 7, 8 The two middle numbers are 7. $(7 + 7) \div 2 = 7$ **Median = 7**
Mode (most frequent):	Find the number or numbers that occur the most. **Mode = 7** If no number occurs the most, then the answer will be "none."

Study the examples above. Then, find the mean, median, and mode of each set of numbers. Round to the nearest tenth.

1. 2, 8, 6, 4, 3, 2, 4

_____

2. 8, 13, 14, 12, 9, 14, 10

_____

3. 23, 22, 28, 26, 18, 20, 25, 23

_____

4. 50, 45, 16, 20, 35, 24

_____

5. 45, 45, 70, 40, 60, 42, 42, 60, 42

_____

6. 71, 62, 58, 34, 43, 56, 12

_____

7. 16, 10, 9, 4, 3, 15, 24, 8, 8, 12

_____

8. 143, 150, 132, 145, 125, 100

_____

Tree Diagrams

A **tree diagram** is used to show the total number of possible outcomes in a probability experiment.

Example: If you flip a coin twice, what are the possible combinations of results?

Heads (H)
H   HH
T   HT

Tails (T)
H   TH
T   TT

Study the example above. Then, draw a tree diagram to illustrate each outcome.

1. choosing chocolate or vanilla ice cream and chocolate or vanilla cake

2. choosing a red or black blouse and a black or white skirt

3. choosing hot cereal or frosted cereal and skim or whole milk

What Is It?

Read the information on the ring-tailed lemur card. Imagine that you are watching a film about animals. Determine whether each animal described could be a ring-tailed lemur. Write *Y* for yes or *N* for no on the line. If your answer is no, highlight the words that explain why.

Ring-Tailed Lemur

Mammal—Primate

Description: Looks like a monkey with a black, pointed snout and has a gray back, a white underside, and a long, bushy tail with black and white rings

Length: 15 inches (excluding tail)

Location: Madagascar, usually on the ground

Diet: Omnivorous—eats primarily fruit, leaves, flowers, and herbs but will also eat insects, small birds, and bird eggs

---

____ **1.** You see an animal that looks like a monkey. Its tail has rings, and it is eating an egg from a nest in the brush.

____ **2.** A second animal arrives and takes the egg away from the first. It, too, looks like a monkey. It has a flat, stubby nose and a long tail with brown and black rings.

____ **3.** A hairy, gray animal is eating fruit and leaves in a tree.

____ **4.** Emerging from behind a termite mound is a three-foot-long animal with a gray back and white underside.

____ **5.** A short-tailed animal with a black, pointed snout is lapping up ants. Its four short legs have black and white rings.

____ **6.** An animal with black and white rings on its tail is sunning itself on the ground.

____ **7.** The carnivorous gray-and-white mammal is slowly stalking a bird in its nest.

Waiting

Read the passage. Use the information to answer the questions.

Audrey stands alone outside by the side of the road, stamping her feet. The sky begins to turn slate gray. She looks longingly at her home. The lit windows smile warmly at her. Audrey rubs her hands together and blows on their bluing tips. "I should have grabbed my mittens," she thinks. A heavy weight rests in the middle of her back: knowledge.

Shivering neighbors slide quietly into a circle of warmth. Too sleepy to talk, they share body warmth and protection from the wind. Barren trees stand guard as they wait. A pair of wide-spaced lights approaches. The circle stirs. It is a false alarm.

A few minutes later, another pair of lights shines like a pair of eyes in the dim light. A welcoming yellow haven stops and opens, admitting the chilly youngsters into humming warmth. It moves along its ebony ribbon between the trees to other cold huddlers and a final destination that will open their minds.

1. What time of day is it? _____

2. Why is Audrey standing by the road? _____

3. Which two words best describe Audrey?

   A. cold and tired   **B.** wise and warm

   C. tired and hungry   **D.** fearful and alert

4. Who are the shivering neighbors? _____

5. What made the circle stir the first time? _____

6. What things do the following phrases describe?

   A. "yellow haven" _____

   B. "destination that will open their minds" _____

   C. "ebony ribbon" _____

   D. "heavy weight . . . in the middle of her back" _____

Matter

As you read the study guide, think of examples of the different states of matter.

- Matter takes up space and has mass.
- There are three states of matter: solid, liquid, and gas.
    solid: is certain size and shape; takes up space; has mass
    liquid: is certain size; takes shape of container; takes up space; has mass
    gas: takes size and shape of container; takes up space; has mass
- Matter has physical properties such as flexibility, color, texture, buoyancy, smell, mass, weight, shape, and size.
- A physical change is a change in shape, size, or state but NOT in type of matter.
- Examples of physical changes to water:
    divide water into two or more containers
    freeze the water (change from liquid to solid)
    melt ice (change from solid to liquid)
    boil water (change from liquid to gas)
    condensation (change from gas to liquid)
    add a substance to it, forming a mixture (examples: adding pepper, rice, etc.)
    crush ice
- A chemical change is a change in type of matter.
  Example: baking a cake
- Two objects cannot occupy the same space at the same time.
- A mixture is a combination of various types of matter in which each maintains its own properties and can be separated out (with tweezers, filter paper, sieve, etc.). Example: trail mix
- A solution is a mixture of two or more substances that cannot be separated by mechanical means (with tweezers, filter paper, sieve, etc.).
- Liquid + liquid: become solution, mix together, or separate into levels
  Examples: food coloring in water and column of liquids
- Solid + liquid: sink, float, melt, dissolve, float, or become soggy
- Determine mass based on the position of a pan on a pan balance or a ruler on a ruler balance.
  Example: The apple has more mass because its pan is lower.

Matter

Use the information on the study guide (page 88) to help you answer the following questions.

1. What two characteristics do all states of matter share?

_____ _____

2. Based on the information given, which state of matter are the following materials?

pepper _____ air _____

apple cider _____ chocolate chip _____

water vapor _____ milk _____

3. Give one more example of each state of matter.

solid: _____ liquid: _____

gas: _____

4. What principle of matter does the following passage demonstrate?

Two students, coming from opposite directions, run around a corner and crash into each other. Both end up staggering backward.

_____

_____

5. Based on the information given, write three physical properties of this paper.

_____ _____ _____

6. List two ways that you could cause a physical change to occur to this paper.

_____ _____

7. Are you made of matter? Give evidence to support your answer.

_____

_____

_____

Time

Solve each problem.

1. Lynn has piano lessons at 2:00 P.M. If her lesson lasts 1 hour, and her trip takes 30 minutes each way, how long is she gone?

    _____

2. Meg gets to work in 45 minutes. Her return trip takes 1 hour and 15 minutes. How long does she travel for work each day?

    _____

3. Zachary wakes up at 6:45 A.M. He eats breakfast at 7:00 A.M. He brushes his teeth at 7:20 A.M. and is on the bus by 7:35 A.M. How long does his entire routine take?

    _____

4. Juan goes to the park at 2:15 P.M. If he returns 3 hours later, what time does he return?

    _____

5. Tracy rides her bike each day for $1\frac{1}{2}$ hours. If she starts at 3:30 P.M., when does she finish?

    _____

6. Darrel arrives at the airport at 2:00 P.M. His flight leaves at 2:45 P.M. The plane lands at 4:15 P.M. How long is his flight?

    _____

7. Sandy leaves her grandparents' house at 4:30 P.M. The trip home takes 2 hours and 40 minutes. What time will she arrive at her home?

    _____

8. Mr. Sellers leaves his office at 9:00 A.M. for a 2-hour meeting. It takes him 45 minutes to travel to or from the meeting place. What time will he return to his office?

    _____

9. Rachel's first class starts at 7:30 A.M. It is 55 minutes long. If her second and third classes are each 55 minutes long, what time will it be at the end of her third class?

    _____

Fractions

> **Trail Mix Recipe**
> (Makes 1 batch.)
>
> $1\frac{1}{4}$ cup sunflower seeds
>
> $1\frac{1}{2}$ cup peanuts
>
> $\frac{3}{4}$ cup candy-coated chocolate pieces
>
> $\frac{5}{8}$ cup raisins

Use the information in the recipe to solve each problem. Write each answer in simplest form.

1. Ellen Johnson planned to make a batch of trail mix, and she wanted to add extra raisins. If she doubled the amount of raisins in the recipe, how many cups of raisins would she need?

2. After measuring the amount of peanuts needed to make a batch of trail mix, Ellen had $2\frac{1}{2}$ cups of peanuts left. How many cups of peanuts did she begin with?

3. Ellen increased the amount of candy-coated chocolate pieces in the recipe to $1\frac{1}{8}$ cups. How many more cups of chocolate pieces did she use than the recipe required?

4. How many cups of trail mix does 1 batch make after all of the ingredients are added together if none of the measurements are altered?

Decimals

Solve each problem.

1. A pipe is 2.7518 cm in diameter. It needs to pass through a hole that is 2.7524 cm. Will it fit? If so, by how much? _____

2. The tax on a soccer ball is $1.32. If the soccer ball costs $22.95, how much money would you need to buy the soccer ball? _____

3. The regular price of a pair of running shoes is $57.45. The shoes are on sale for $43.95. How much will you save by buying the shoes on sale? _____

4. Stacy bought a poster for $3.95 and a CD for $11.95. How much did she spend altogether? _____

These squares are called "magic squares" because each column, row, and diagonal adds to the same "magic sum." Complete each magic square.

5.

	a.	
1.05		2.73
b.	c.	d.
e.		
1.47		3.15

Magic Sum = __6.3__

6.

	f.	g.
0.65		
	h.	i.
	1.35	
	j.	
0.37		0.93

Magic Sum = _____

Page 14: 1. D., E.; **2.** C., F.;
3. B., H.; **4.** A., G.

Page 15: Topic: Machines
need energy to work.;
Main Idea: Energy comes
from many sources.;
1. fossil fuels; A. come
from earth; B. fuel power
plants, automobiles,
other machines; **2.** wind;
A. powers windmills; B. is
converted into electricity,
pushes gears, or pumps
water; **3.** water; A. dams
used to converted
energy into electricity;
B. possibility of using
ocean waves and tides;
4. solar energy; A. solar
cells change sunlight into
electricity; B. power cars
and electrical devices
and heat homes

Page 17: main idea—
vertebrates are animals
that do not have
backbones. major
details—Order will vary
but should include:
amphibians, birds, fish,
mammals, reptiles.;
minor supporting details:
Answers will vary. Accept
any reasonable answer.

Page 18: 1. 40; 700;
2,000; **2.** 5; 800,000;
70,000,000; **3.** 9,000;
600,000; 7,000,000; **4.** 300;
40,000,000; 20,000; **5.** 30;
900,000,000; 1,000,000;
6. Answers will vary.

Page 19: 1. 2,000; **2.** 5,000;
3. 2,000; **4.** 300,000; **5.** 400;
6. 50,000; **7.** 600,000;
8. 50,000; **9.** 50,000; **10.** 2

Page 20: 1. 36, 144, 28,
324; **2.** 192; 1440; 288, 127;
3. 18; 10,560; 6, 10; **4.** 4, 17;
7,920; 8; **5.** 12 yd. 1 ft.; 2
yd. 1 ft.; 7 yd. 1 ft.; 2 yd. 1
ft.; **6.** 2 ft. 4 in.; 3 ft. 9 in.; 18
ft. 9 in.; 20 ft. 6 in.

Page 21: 1. 1; **2.** 5; **3.** 2;
4. 2; **5.** 3; **6.** 6; **7.** 7,000;
160; 800; **8.** 110; 5; 7;
9. 4; 12,000; 8; **10.** 170;
350; 6,800;

Page 22: 1. B.; **2.** A.; **3.** C.;
4. B.; **5.** A.; **6.** A.

Page 23: 1. B.; **2.** C.; **3.** B.;
4. A.; **5.** A.; **6.** C.; **7.** A.;
8. B.; **9.** B.; **10.** C.

Page 24: 1. Juan pushes
the swing.; **2.** Tien
continues in a back and
forward arc.; **3.** She bumps
the bag.; **4.** It explodes.;
5.–6. Answers will vary.

Page 25: Answers will
vary but should follow a
logical order.

Page 26: 1. 67; 776;
1,164; 553; **2.** 794; 982;
1,262; 1,516; **3.** 2,119;
4,643; 4,339; 16,519;
4. 11,601; 10,062; 10,756;
7,959; **5.** 66,344; 109,018;
42,402; 82,780

Page 27: 1. 8, 4; 7, 11; 6,
8; **2.** 7, 8; 5, 15; 7, 9; **3.** Y
= 3, x = 16, v = 10, m = 6;
4. c = 6, n = 12, h = 18, s
= 16; **5.** a = 13, w = 9, g =
16, p = 18

Page 28: 1. 123; 222; 314;
65; 614; **2.** 401; 81; 188;

387; 397; **3.** 7,273; 4,121;
1,900; 1,058; 437; **4.** 8,530;
4,629; 7,801; 1,289; 1,491

Page 29: 1. 6, 11; 8, 15; 8,
21; **2.** 25, 42; 62, 187; 20,
120; **3.** g = 56, x = 36, j = 26,
m = 28; **4.** q = 115, r = 56, w
= 64, z = 41; **5.** y = 167, h =
25, a = 36, c = 107

Page 30: 1. B.; **2.** C.; **3.** B.;
4. A.; **5.** A.

Page 31: 1. Don't look a
gift horse in the mouth.;
2. A penny saved is a
penny earned.; **3.** A miss
is as good as a mile.;
4. Don't make a mountain
out of a molehill.; **5.** A fool
and his money are soon
parted.; **Extra:** Hitch your
wagon to a star.

Page 33: 1. Iesha; **2.** Iesha;
3. Jackie; **4.** Jackie; **5.** both;
6. Jackie; **7.** both;
Answers will vary.

Page 34: 1. 0, zero;
2. 6, 3, 4, associative;
3. 7, 8, commutative;
4. 6, commutative;
5. 7, 4, associative; **6.** 0,
zero; **7.** 1, identity; **8.** 5,
9, associative; **9.** 241,
identity; **10.** 9, 4, 9, 3,
distributive; **11.** 3, 12, 3, 10,
distributive

Page 35: 1. 8, 9; 9, 9; 6, 7;
2. 7, 5; 5, 10; 7, 8; **3.** x = 4,
v = 4, h = 8, g = 3; **4.** n =
8, j = 2, t = 5, d = 10; **5.** b
= 4, f = 17, c = 12, r = 13

Page 36: 1. 867, 422, 112
r2, 113 r4; **2.** 211 r4, 270
r4, 913 r1, 512 r2; **3.** 311
r7, 712 r1, 650 r1, 214 r1

Page 37: 1. 9, 36; 8, 56; 4, 64; **2.** 18, 450; 16, 384; 12, 180; **3.** b = 49, p = 24, t = 63, j= 42; **4.** c = 50, g = 36, y = 1,875, s = 242; **5.** w = 918, k = 540, d = 492, z = 464

Page 38: 1. Main Idea: household measuring tools; Nonsupportive Detail: Carpets help keep your feet warm.; **2.** Main Idea: rain forest plants; Nonsupportive Detail: Rain forests have animals, like monkeys and sloths.; **3.** Main Idea: Computers have many uses; Nonsupportive Detail: Computers even come in many different colors.; **4.** Main Idea: superstitions; Nonsupportive Detail: Many people think that superstitions are silly.; **5.** Main Idea: People react differently to anesthesia.; Nonsupportive Detail: Anesthesia makes surgery easy for people because they don't experience any pain.; **6.** Main Idea: Limiting television viewing time is important.; Nonsupportive Detail: Watching educational television is better than watching horror shows.

Page 39: 1. B.; **2.** A.; **3.** C.

Page 41: Answers will vary.

Page 42: 1. 6: 1, 2, 3, 6; 18: 1, 2, 3, 6, 9, 18; GCF = 6; 4: 1, 2, 4; 12: 1, 2, 3, 4, 6, 12; GCF = 4; **2.** 12: 1, 2, 3, 4, 6, 12; 18: 1, 2, 3, 6, 9, 18; GCF = 6; 14: 1, 2, 7, 14; 21: 1,

3, 7, 21; GCF = 7; **3.** 18: 1, 2,3, 6, 9, 18; 27: 1, 3, 9, 27; GCF = 9; 24: 1, 2, 3, 4, 6, 8, 12, 24; 32: 1, 2, 4, 8, 16, 32; GCF = 8; **4.** 9: 1, 3, 9; 12: 1, 2, 3, 4, 6, 12; GCF = 3; 9: 1, 3, 9; 15: 1, 3, 5, 15; GCF = 3; **5.** 15: 1, 3, 5, 15; 20: 1, 2, 4, 5, 10, 20; GCF = 5; 15: 1, 3, 5, 15; 40: 1, 2, 4, 5, 8, 10, 20, 40; GCF = 5; **6.** 14: 1, 2, 7, 14; 35: 1, 5, 7, 35; GCF = 7; 15: 1, 3, 5, 15; 35: 1, 5, 7, 35; GCF = 5

Page 43: 1. 6: 6, 12, 18, 24 …, 2: 2, 4, 6, 8 …, LCM = 6; 4: 4, 8, 12, 16 …, 8: 8, 16, 24, 32 …, LCM = 8; **2.** 5: 5, 10, 15, 20, 25 …, 3: 3, 6, 9, 12, 15 …, LCM = 15; 4: 4, 8, 12, 16 …, 6: 6, 12, 18, 24 …, LCM = 12; **3.** 8: 8, 16, 24, 32 …, 12: 12, 24, 36, 48 …, LCM = 24; 6: 6, 12, 18, 24, 30 …, 10: 10, 20, 30, 40, 50…, LCM = 30; **4.** 6: 6, 12, 18, 24, 30, 36 …, 5: 5, 10, 15, 20, 25, 30 …, 15: 15, 30, 45, 60, 75, 90 …, LCM = 30; 4: 4, 8, 12, 16, 20, 24, 28, 32, 36 …, 9: 9, 18, 27, 36, 45 …, 18: 18, 36, 54 …, LCM = 36; **5.** 8: 8, 16, 24, 32, 40 …, 10: 10, 20, 30, 40, 50 …, 20: 20, 40, 60, 80, 100 …, LCM = 40, 10: 10, 20, 30, 40 …, 15: 15, 30, 45 …, 30: 30, 60, 90 …, LCM = 30

Page 44: 1. $\frac{1}{9}, \frac{3}{9}, \frac{2}{6}, \frac{1}{6}, \frac{25}{30}, \frac{12}{30}$; **2.** $\frac{12}{24}, \frac{16}{24}, \frac{6}{18}, \frac{6}{18}, \frac{36}{45}, \frac{15}{45}$; **3.** $\frac{14}{28}, \frac{12}{28}, \frac{16}{24}, \frac{18}{24}, \frac{18}{30}, \frac{25}{30}$

Page 45: 1. =, >, >, <; **2.** >, <, >, >; **3.** <, >, =, <; **4.** $\frac{1}{3}, \frac{7}{12}, \frac{3}{4}, \frac{5}{6}$; **5.** $\frac{3}{7}, \frac{1}{2}, \frac{3}{4}, \frac{5}{6}$

Page 46: 6, 5, 2, 7, 4, 1, 3

Page 47: 6, 4, 1, 3, 5, 7, 2

Page 49: 1. a bad day; **2.** He didn't pick up the penny.; **3.** a good day; **4.** the penny; **5.** Answers will vary.; 7, 6, 3, 2, 1, 5, 4

Page 50: 1. $\frac{1}{40}, \frac{1}{28}, \frac{1}{96}$; **2.** $\frac{12}{35}, \frac{3}{5}, \frac{8}{21}$; **3.** $\frac{2}{3}, \frac{7}{12}, \frac{56}{81}$; **4.** $\frac{1}{2}, \frac{2}{9}, \frac{3}{16}$; **5.** $\frac{21}{50}, \frac{10}{49}, \frac{4}{9}$; **6.** $\frac{9}{28}, \frac{5}{12}, \frac{5}{12}$

Page 51: 1. $\frac{5}{11}, \frac{4}{9}, \frac{1}{9}, 3\frac{1}{3}, \frac{3}{26}$; **2.** $7\frac{8}{37}, \frac{11}{15}, 6\frac{2}{9}$; **3.** $1\frac{1}{3}, \frac{1}{3}, \frac{4}{9}, \frac{8}{61}, 1$; **4.** $\frac{3}{17}, 1\frac{2}{7}, \frac{1}{27}, \frac{5}{11}, \frac{5}{17}$

Page 52: 1. 7, 2, 2; **2.** $13\frac{1}{2}, 6\frac{2}{3}, 8\frac{3}{4}$; **3.** $1\frac{1}{2}, \frac{1}{2}, \frac{3}{10}, \frac{5}{3}$; **4.** 5, $2, \frac{5}{6}, \frac{3}{5}$; **5.** $2\frac{1}{2}, 1\frac{11}{24}, 1\frac{1}{6}, 1\frac{1}{7}$

Page 53: 1. n = $\frac{2}{5}$, n = $\frac{2}{3}$, n = $2\frac{2}{9}$; **2.** n = 1; n = $\frac{8}{15}$, n = $2\frac{1}{4}$; **3.** n = $\frac{1}{3}$, n = $2\frac{1}{4}$, n = $13\frac{1}{3}$; **4.** n = $2\frac{1}{3}$, n = $5\frac{1}{3}$, n = 21; **5.** n = $36\frac{3}{4}$, n = 25, n = 6

Page 55: 1. C.; **2.** D.; **3.** B.; **4.** A.; **5.** B.

Page 57: 1. bones losing mass and becoming more likely to break or fracture; **2.** collapsed vertebrae, incredible back pain, spinal deformities; **3.** because kids do not get enough calcium and if they do not grow enough bone, it cannot be rebuilt; **4.** by the age of 18; **5.** It has calcium.; **6.** can eat other dairy products or green vegetables; **7.** It leaches calcium from the bones.; **8.** exercise, eat a balanced diet, do not smoke; **9.** Answers will vary.

Page 58: 1. 141.37, 40, 15.3; **2.** 4.297, 0.1, 27.79; **3.** 546.08, 3.2, 13.08; **4.** 444, 4.1, 607.8; **5.** 16.654, 67.3, 6; **6.** 2.76, 5.5, 6.29; **7.** 21, 99.4, 635.682; **8.** 59.6, 18, 53.6; **9.** 1.27 days

Page 59: 1. 1.37, 13.48, 12.013, 54.543, 122.218; **2.** 914.064, 171.369, 153.703, 70.027, 48.07; **3.** 1.29, 707.414, 495.723, 282.793, 525.425; **4.** 254.587, 138.281, 19.64, 9.932, 239.163; **5.** 171.473, 105.003, 25.127; **6.** 83.118, 245.554, 834.243

Page 60: 1. 0.00182, 0.000504, 0.00387, 0.001; **2.** 0.001749, 0.000672, 0.00244, 0.00315; **3.** 0.0132, 0.0194, 0.015, 0.02451; **4.** 0.007912, 0.002875, 0.003901, 0.02781; **5.** 0.000515, 0.00289, 0.003552, 0.000682

Page 61: 1. 0.7, 0.08, 0.009, 0.07; **2.** 0.065, 0.02375, 0.0902, 0.01775; **3.** 0.00625, 0.03, 6.24, 0.006; **4.** 0.0207, 0.035, 3.5, 0.033

Page 63: E, F, H, I, D, A, G, J, C, B; **1.** solid, liquid, gas; **2.** Answers will vary but

may include: rivers, glaciers, and oceans.; **3.** snow, rain; **4.** Answers will vary but may include: drinking, bathing, cooking, and growing plants.; **5.** salt; **6.** heat, wind, and increased surface area

Page 64: 7. B.; **8.** C.; **9.** B.; **10.** A.; **11.** B.; **12.** B.; **13.** B.; **14.** C.; **15.** B.; A. water as a gas; B. Water vapor rises and cools, condensing on particles, like dust. Millions of these drops form clouds.

Page 65: 1. excited and happy; **2.** irritated and crabby; **3.** frogs began croaking, ducks began quacking, the wind was blowing, waves came on shore

Page 66: 1. $\overleftrightarrow{CD}$ or $\overleftrightarrow{DC}$; $\overleftrightarrow{KL}$; $\overleftrightarrow{MN}$ or $\overleftrightarrow{NM}$; $\overleftrightarrow{TU}$ or $\overleftrightarrow{UT}$; **2.** $\overrightarrow{RV}$ or $\overrightarrow{VR}$; $\overleftrightarrow{EF}$; $\overleftrightarrow{AZ}$; $\overrightarrow{JI}$ or $\overrightarrow{IJ}$; **3.** $\overleftrightarrow{XY}$ or $\overleftrightarrow{YX}$; $\overleftrightarrow{PQ}$ or $\overleftrightarrow{QP}$; $\overrightarrow{GH}$; $\overleftrightarrow{YZ}$ or $\overleftrightarrow{ZY}$

Page 67: 1. 4.; **2.** 7.; **3.** 1.; **4.** 5.; **5.** 9.; **6.** 3.; **7.** 8.; **8.** 6.; **9.** 2.

Page 68: 1. ∠ABC or ∠CBA, right; ∠MPV or ∠VPM, acute; ∠CJG or ∠GJC, obtuse; ∠AVW or ∠WVA, right; **2.** ∠DMS or ∠SMD, acute; ∠ABR or ∠RBA, obtuse; ∠LMN or ∠NML, right; ∠IKJ or ∠JKI, obtuse

Page 69: 1. P = 20 m, A = 25 m²; **2.** P = 28 m, A = 40

m²; **3.** P = 84 cm, A = 300 cm²; **4.** P = 24 cm, A = 36 cm²; **5.** P = 76 m, A = 320 m²; **6.** P = 48 yd, A = 80 yd²; **7.** P = 36 ft., A = 81 ft²; **8.** P = 110 ft., A = 400 ft²

Page 71: 1. C.; **2.** A.; **3.** C.; **4.** C.; **5.** A.; **6.** B.; **7.** Answers will vary.

Page 73: 1. reoccurring; **2.** interconnecting passageways that let oxygen and carbon dioxide pass between the body and the outside air; **3.** the bronchi squeeze too tightly, and the brachial tree produces too much mucus, which traps carbon dioxide; **4.** what causes airway to constrict and produce more mucus; **5.** allergens, irritants, virus, bacteria, exercise, stress

Page 74: 1. $\frac{4}{6}$, 4:6, 4 to 6; **2.** $\frac{10}{9}$, 10:9, 10 to 9; **3.** $\frac{5}{7}$, 5:7, 5 to 7; **4.** $\frac{3}{4}$, 3:4, 3 to 4; **5.** $\frac{5}{4}$, 5:4, 5 to 4; **6.** $\frac{12}{18}$, 12:18, 12 to 18; **7.** $\frac{6}{11}$, 6:11, 6 to 11; **8.** $\frac{13}{15}$, 13:15, 13 to 15; **9.** $\frac{11}{23}$, 11:23, 11 to 23; **10.** $\frac{12}{23}$, 12:23, 12 to 23; **11.** $\frac{1}{26}$, 1:26, 1 to 26; **12.** $\frac{3}{950}$, 3:950, 3 to 950; **13.** $\frac{2}{5}$, 2:5, 2 to 5; **14.** $\frac{18}{9}$, 18:9, 18 to 9; **15.** $\frac{3}{4}$, 3:4, 3 to 4; **16.** $\frac{7}{8}$, 7:8, 7 to 8; **17.** girls

Page 75: 1. no, yes, no; **2.** yes, yes, yes; **3.** no, yes, no; **4.** x = 30, x = 6, x = 12; **5.** x = 15, x = 3, x = 16; **6.** x = 24, x = 15, x = 12

Answer Key

Page 76: 1. 29%, 61%, 8%, 25%; **2.** 5%, 85%, 97%, 67%; **3.** 40%, 13%, 51%,75%; **4.** $\frac{1}{2}$, $\frac{3}{10}$, $\frac{1}{4}$, $\frac{1}{5}$; **5.** $\frac{73}{100}$, $\frac{16}{25}$, $\frac{3}{20}$, $\frac{2}{5}$; **6.** $\frac{3}{5}$, $\frac{33}{100}$, $\frac{3}{4}$, $\frac{1}{10}$; **7.** $\frac{63}{100}$, $\frac{19}{20}$, $\frac{7}{10}$, $\frac{43}{50}$; **8.** Answers will vary.

Page 77: 1. 12, 2, 6; **2.** 3.6, 20, 3; **3.** 5, 7.2, 3; **4.** 24.5, 18, 27; **5.** 8, 10.4, 2; **6.** 40, 15.5, 27; **7.** 15, 44, 66; **8.** =, <, >

Page 78: 1. at the Field Museum in Chicago, in the past; **2.** on a trail in a wagon on the way to California, in the past; **3.** in her bedroom in Idaho, in the future; **4.** in the woods in Oregon, in the present

Page 79: 1. present, Answers will vary.; **2.** past, Answers will vary.; **3.** present, Answers will vary.; **4.** future, Answers will vary.

Page 80: 1. the side of a road in a milkweed patch; **2.** Audrey, Jade; **3.** Audrey needs four more caterpillars for school.; **4.-5.** Answers will vary.

Page 81: 1. Porchia has to clean her room, but the movie will start soon.; **2.** Tony is skating in a dangerous way.; **3.** Darryl wants to try out for the play, but he doesn't have a ride home.; **4.** Ana cannot wear her sweater because the button came off.; **5.** Eric does not have enough money to buy an MP3 player.

Page 82: 1. $\frac{1}{2}$; **2.** $\frac{1}{2}$; **3.** $\frac{1}{3}$; **4.** $\frac{2}{3}$; **5.** $\frac{1}{6}$; **6.** 1; **7.** $\frac{1}{52}$; **8.** $\frac{1}{52}$; **9.** $\frac{1}{26}$; **10.** $\frac{1}{13}$; **11.** $\frac{1}{2}$; **12.** $\frac{2}{13}$; **13.** $\frac{1}{4}$; **14.** $\frac{1}{26}$

Page 83: 1. 9, 5, 7; **2.** 5.6, 8.3, 8.4; **3.** 7.2, 8, 10; **4.** 10.3, 11.4, 7.4; **5.** 348.7, 99.8, 79.5; **6.** 134.7, 79.3, 89

Page 84: 1. mean 4.1, median 4, mode 2 and 4; **2.** mean 11.4, median 12, mode 14; **3.** mean 23.1, median 23, mode 23; **4.** mean 31.7, median 29.5, mode none; **5.** mean 49.6, median 45, mode 42; **6.** mean 48, median 56, mode none; **7.** mean 10.9, median 9.5, mode 8; **8.** mean 132.5, median 137.5, mode none

Page 85:
1. 4 outcomes
chocolate ice cream — chocolate cake, vanilla cake
vanilla ice cream — chocolate cake, vanilla cake

2. 4 outcomes
red blouse — black skirt, white skirt
black blouse — black skirt, white skirt

3. 4 outcomes
hot cereal — skim milk, whole milk
frosted cereal — skim milk, whole milk

Page 86: 1. Y; **2.** N; **3.** N; **4** N; **5.** N; **6.** Y; **7.** N

Page 87: 1. early morning; **2.** waiting for the bus; **3.** A; **4.** other kids waiting for the bus; **5.** they thought a car was the bus; **6.** school bus, school, the road, backpack

Page 89: 1. have mass, take up space; **2.** From left to right and top to bottom: solid, gas, liquid, solid, gas, liquid; **3.** Answers will vary.; **4.** Two objects cannot occupy the same space at the same time.; **5.** Answers will vary but may include: solid, has shape, is black and white; **6.** put it in water, cut it in half; **7.** Yes, I have mass and take up space.

Page 90: 1. 2 hours; **2.** 2 hours; **3.** 50 minutes; **4.** 5:15 PM; **5.** 5:00 PM; **6.** 1 hour and 30 minutes or 1.5 hours; **7.** 7:10 PM; **8.** 12:30 PM; **9.** 10:15 AM

Page 91: 1. 1 1/4 cups of raisins; **2.** 4 cups of peanuts; **3.** 3/8 cup of chocolate pieces; **4.** 4 1/8 cups of trail mix

Page 92: 1. yes, by 0.0006 cm; **2.** $24.27; **3.** $13.50; **4.** $15.90; **5.** from left to right and top to bottom: 2.52, 3.78, 2.1, 0.42, 1.68; **6.** from left to right and top to bottom: 0.51, 1.21, 0.79, 0.23, 1.07, 2.37